Sumo Wrestlers & Supermodels

What 20 Years of Teaching Has Taught Me About Saving Black Children From American Schools

By Joel I. Plummer

Cover art by Lyle Omolayo
www.lyleomolayo.com

Plummer Media & Entertainment, LLC.

1424 East 7th Street

Plainfield, NJ 07062

www.joelplummer.com

Paperback ISBN: 978-0-9744490-8-1

To Alexis, Morgan, and Mason,

Hopefully, by the time you can understand this book, you will live in a world where people no longer debate your humanity. If not, pick up where I left off and continue the fight.

Prologue

There is a myth in academia called academic objectivity–
the idea that scholars are to be neutral in their research
and presentation of information. If you picked up this
volume looking for that, you chose the wrong book. I am a
Black teacher and the father of three Black children–I have
no neutral stances on the education of my children who
live in a society that still questions their complete
humanity. Every single word I write about Black children
and education is personal for me. Every thought I have
about how schools educate Black children has life and
death implications for my own children and millions of
other Black children throughout the nation. I do not intend
for this book to be a "balanced" look at how schools
educate Black children. There should be no balance
between racist educational practices and non-racist ones.

For more than twenty years, I have operated in the
classroom as if I am in the middle of a war because I am–it
is the war for Black children's minds and bodies. From the
founding of the Jamestown colony in 1619 to the Civil Rights
Act of 1968, it took America 349 years to even loosely
profess that Black people are full human beings that should
have equal rights in America. That means Black people
have been legally subhuman in America for about 300
more years than have been legally recognized as full human
beings. In a country that has White supremacy so
embedded into its foundation, there is no way that its
schools can avoid replicating the same racist practices and
beliefs that the larger society contains. Schools should be
the most powerful tool in the fight to eliminate White

supremacist thought in America, but sadly, too often, they become places that overtly and covertly perpetuate it.

From the outset, let me unequivocally state that all kids are not the same, and the construct of race absolutely matters in education. So-called "color-blind" education is a dangerous tool of White supremacist oppression that Black children should avoid at all costs. This entire book's premise is that Black children are not the same as White children in America and their unique socio-historical experiences require a unique approach to their schooling. The current one-size-fits-all American education model is absolutely disastrous for Black children. Educating Black students in the same manner as White students is as futile as training both a sumo wrestler and a supermodel in identical ways. If you train a sumo wrestler the way you do a supermodel, that sumo wrestler will get destroyed when they apply that training to their real world circumstances. If you train a supermodel the same way you train a sumo wrestler, they will be a spectacular failure in their world as well. Black people are getting obliterated in America today precisely because American schools have educated them to think and act in ways that do not address their unique problems and circumstances.

If you picked up this book because you were intrigued by the title and want to cheat, you can go straight to chapter 7, where I go into depth about my sumo wrestlers & supermodels analogy. I would encourage you, however, to read this book in its entirety to understand the full context of that analogy. As a whole, this book represents the critical insights I gained during my career that I argue teachers and parents should possess to combat the one-size-fits-all model of American education that schools subject Black children to and all the pieces matter.

Many people profess to be education experts who validate their claims by pointing to the number of degrees they possess or considerable amounts of research attached to their names. Those people should be commended for their work, but it is also important to note that many of those people would struggle to survive two days, let alone two decades, teaching where I have worked. That is why this text exists. I wanted to create a book for future teachers and parents of Black children based on real-life experience. Everything I write about in this book is what I have actually done and experienced with a great deal of success.

Each chapter is a separate lesson that anyone working with Black children needs to know. Some of the lessons are long and detailed, while others are a mere few sentences. No matter the length, each chapter represents a critical piece of understanding that has enabled me to teach successfully.

What you will not find here is hundreds of pages of empirical studies on Black children and education. Instead, what you will find is the accumulated wisdom from being on the frontlines of Black urban education for more than twenty years. There is value in the work of a scholar who can explain the larger context of a war and its implications. But there is also incredible value in the story of the soldier who was actually in the war and experienced the consequences of every single decision that was made in it. So even though these are the thoughts of one educator, I hope that they will resonate with readers and, at the very least, provide an individual data point for those that are doing broader studies of teacher effectiveness with Black students.

On a final, personal note, this book also represents my acknowledgment that my time on this Earth as an educator is minuscule in the scope of history. Like all teachers, no matter their level of effectiveness, someday I will retire, and within a year or so, my complete existence will be forgotten. All of the work a teacher does in a school eventually exits the building in an annual event called graduation. When even the greatest of teachers retire, they generally are forgotten. Within a year or two, even their former colleagues no longer mention their name. Because this is the case, master teachers usually leave very few breadcrumbs for the educators who follow them. This book is an attempt to stop that cycle.

I remember being told once that a great leader makes themselves obsolete. If a leader has the proper impact on an organization, it should still run in their absence. People usually create permanent institutions to immortalize and perpetuate the goals and work of visionaries and leaders. In this way, even if a great leader leaves, it is of little consequence because there is a permanent structure in place that perpetually replicates the original leader's success.

My ego is not so grandiose that I think an entire institution needs to be erected dedicated to my beliefs on teaching. However, I hope that this book can serve the same function as an institution in that even after I am long gone, the words in this volume will help future teachers and parents of Black children replicate the success that I have had in the classroom.

What follows is a collection of knowledge that has yielded me success during my years fighting in the war to save Black children's minds. I hope that it is a welcomed addition to the work that is already being done in the struggle to make American schools effectively teach all of its students.

Lesson 1: What is an Education?

We cannot begin to discuss how to most effectively teach Black children without first defining what an education is. Historian, John Henrik Clarke (1995), summarized that "the main purpose of education is to train the student to be a proper handler of power. Every form of true education trains the student in self-reliance" (p. 165). The goal of education, then, is not knowledge for knowledge's sake. The goal of education is power. *Power* is a group's capacity to define, defend, and develop its interests even in the face of opposition (Karenga, 2002). If we accept these definitions of education and power. In that case, we can clearly see that, en masse, systems of learning designed by White people have yielded Black students none of those things.

> *The goal of education, then, is not knowledge for knowledge's sake. The goal of education is power.*

Instead of receiving an education, Black students generally receive training. Training and education are related but they are very different from each other (Akbar, 1998). *Training* is the action of teaching a person or animal a particular skill or type of behavior. For generations, schools have not taught Black students how to explain who they are, advance their self-interests, and value and protect those interests. For example, at the time of this writing, mass protests are happening over continued incidents of police violence involving Black people in America. Even though there are, collectively, thousands of Black legal scholars, lawyers, judges, and elected officials, the American justice system continually denies its Black citizens justice. America's denial of justice to the Black community is partially the result of Black students receiving training instead of education. American schools trained them on how to maintain the existing system—not overthrow it. No one should condemn people who have tried to do good work within the system. They face the same challenge that all Black people face in American institutions: The path to success in America usually maintains its current systems and rewards people for minimizing reformers and eliminating revolutionaries. Nevertheless, this is all rooted in powerlessness, and a people with no power cannot consider themselves educated.

Lesson 2: The Mismatch of European Education Systems and Black Students

The most important factor in the success of a teacher is how well they know their students. But knowing your students means more than being familiar with who they are and how they live currently. To successfully teach Black students, you need to have some understanding of the full historical journey that ended with that student sitting in your classroom. So to even begin to understand the challenges that face Black students, we must first do a brief survey of the historical problems of Black students in learning systems designed by White people. When we do that, one of the themes that will arise is that even in the 21st Century, the education delivered to Black students has rarely been for their benefit.

European invaders in Africa established schools that they designed to make African students loyal to European interests, ideals, and mores even when they were obviously counter to their self-interests. The colonization of a people is not possible unless the colonizers convince them they are incapable of ruling themselves. Then, the question becomes, "How does one rule a people, and make them like it?" Europeans realized that the most efficient way to rule Africans was not through regulating their bodies, but through the control of their minds. If Europeans could get Africans to accept and even believe in the European vision of what Africans were and should be, they would not have to rely so heavily on military strength to control them. If they could make Africans internalize European perceptions of themselves and their land, Africans would police themselves.

To gain control of Africans' minds, Europeans started an intense pro-European propaganda campaign. Europeans subjected Africans to brainwashing experiences through Christian missionaries and colonial schools. Europeans designed colonial schools to maintain the unequal power relationship between hegemonic and oppressed groups, not to challenge them. Walter Rodney wrote that the colonial school system's main purpose was to train Africans to help Europeans maintain control of their African colonies (1996). Europeans did not design the colonial education system to empower Africans to become successful rulers of their destinies. Europeans' intent for the colonial education system in Africa was to do just the opposite. "Its goal was to make its students snub their noses at all that was African, and to worship all that was European and capitalist. Colonial schooling was education for subordination, exploitation, the creation of mental confusion, and the development of underdevelopment" (Rodney, 1996, p. 209).

Colonial schooling was education for subordination, exploitation, the creation of mental confusion, and the development of underdevelopment.

The colonial schools Europeans established in Africa taught Africans to perform menial jobs such as junior clerks and messengers. The prevailing thought by the schools' administrators was that too much learning would be wasted on Africans. Africans did not need to learn anything beyond what was necessary for them to keep track of and deliver packages. Thus, Europeans put little money into African education relative to non-African students. In 1959, Uganda spent eleven pounds per year on each African child for education while spending one hundred and eighty-six pounds on each European child (Rodney, 1996).

More damaging than being only trained to perform menial tasks was colonial schools' practice of teaching African students that their history and culture were insignificant. For instance, African students in a constant tropical climate learned about the four seasons, rivers, lakes, and mountains in Europe, but nothing of African bodies of water and mountain ranges.

Schools in British colonies in Africa taught their students to write statements such as "we defeated the Spanish Armada in 1588" at a time when Hawkins was stealing Africans and being knighted by Queen Elizabeth I for so doing" (Rodney, 1996, p. 210). The schools for African students in French colonies taught them that their ancestors had blue eyes and that Napoleon was their greatest general. Rodney points out that this is an amazing proclamation coming from Africans' mouths, considering that Napoleon reinstituted slavery in Guadeloupe and tried, but failed, to do the same in Haiti (Rodney, 1996). Thus, self-hate was inherent in the education that Africans received in colonial schools because the system attempted to Europeanize the African, and if one was European, they could not also be African (Rodney, 1996).

Rodney points out that not all colonial administrators were consciously trying to corrode Africans' minds so they could be more easily controlled and exploited. "On the contrary," he writes, "most of them thought they were doing the African a great favor" (Rodney, 1996, p. 211). Nonetheless, the reality of the situation was that the African mind was being weakened and supplanted with racist European notions of the world despite any good intentions.

Lesson 3: America Education as a Tool of Control

Just as in Africa, in America, the education that Black learners have received at the hands of White people has been problematic since its inception. Much of the schooling that Black Americans have received incorporates many of the debilitating and detrimental practices of colonial Africa's educational system in lieu of a proper education.

As long as Black people have been in America, they have struggled to receive an education that serves them positively and meaningfully. During slavery, some states felt it necessary to officially ban teaching slaves to read and write. Some Southerners viewed a literate slave population as rebellious and dangerous, and thus they viewed the teaching of enslaved Black people to read as a criminal act. Frederick Douglass, in his classic work, *The Narrative of the Life of Frederick Douglass,* gave a clear example of how important it was for slave owners to hold their "property" in a state of ignorance. The wife of Frederick Douglass' enslaver began to teach him how to read, but her husband cut his learning short when he found out:

> ...Mr. Auld found out what was going on, and at once forbade Mrs. Auld to instruct me further, telling her, among other things, that it was unlawful, as well as unsafe, to teach a slave to read. To use his own words, further he said, "If you give a nigger an inch, he will take an ell. A nigger should know nothing but to obey his master to do as he is told to do. Learning would spoil the best nigger in the world. Now," said he "if you teach that nigger (speaking of

7

myself) how to read, there would be no keeping him. It would forever unfit him to be a slave. He would at once become unmanageable, and of no value to his master. As to himself, it could do him no good, but a great deal of harm. It would make him discontented and unhappy" (qtd. in Gates, 1987, pp. 274-275).

Illiteracy was a powerful weapon in slave owners' fight to control the behavior of enslaved Black people. By denying enslaved Black people the ability to read, slave owners, stifled their ability to discover any alternatives to their current lives. Slave owners' fears were not unfounded as enslaved Black people that could read and write were active in slave rebellions in both the 1700s and 1800s (Walker, 1992). Despite laws that prohibited the schooling of enslaved Black people, they still received a formal and systematic education. Unfortunately, the education they received was based on a curriculum of subjugation. European and American slavers had to teach captured Africans how to be slaves in America. There was nothing inherent in Africans or their culture that would make them willing participants in their oppression in the new world. The only way that the American slave system could possibly work was to reeducate the captured Africans to make them believe that they were inferior and deserving of their lot as slaves. White slave owners' reprogramming of enslaved Africans' minds required that they expose them to a system of education that was intentionally demeaning and

Despite laws that prohibited the schooling of enslaved Black people, they still received a formal and systematic education. Unfortunately, the education they received was based on a curriculum of subjugation.

humiliating. Slave owners taught enslaved Africans to believe that they had, at best, a weak claim to humanity, with no noteworthy history or culture, and no hopes of attaining either outside of adopting that of White Americans' (Anderson, 1992).

The process of "educating" captured Africans to become submissive slaves usually involved five steps:

1. Make slaves understand that they must obey at all times. The slightest opposition to the White power structure must be put down immediately.

2. Make slaves believe that they are personally inferior. Enslaved Africans have to be made to feel that their history and culture taint them.

3. Awe slaves with a sense of their White master's power.

4. Make slaves think that their interests are connected to their White master's interests.

5. Make slaves believe that they are helpless. Slaves have to be taught that they can do nothing of value apart from White people (Stampp, 1956).

After the demise of slavery in America, Black people made limited progress attaining a quality education. Famed historian, Carter G. Woodson, explained that though Black people were physically emancipated, they were yet to be set free from the intellectual bondage placed on them by White people during slavery and the Jim Crow era. Woodson argued that the curriculum that Black students were exposed to neither prepared them to handle the challenges of being Black in America nor did it sufficiently combat the centuries of White supremacist thought that made Black people feel inferior and White people feel falsely superior (Woodson, 2000).

In the next chapter, we will examine the context of the world in which those early Black schools were forced to operate and how the unique challenges Black people faced after slavery shaped the type of education Black people would receive for the next century.

Lesson 4: The Missing Link

We must spend some time here in the period after slavery. It is impossible to understand modern America and, by extension, its schools without understanding how race and White supremacy shaped the nation. What follows is the context in which the first Black schools were created and operated. An examination of this period will make it overwhelmingly clear why Black schools have been unavoidably problematic from their inception.

Many students have at least a basic understanding of what happened in the civil rights movement of the 1950s and 1960s. However, few of my students know the details of what Black leaders were fighting for beyond minutia like using the same water fountains and toilets as White people. While just about everybody in America has some familiarity with the American slave system (or at the very least, they recognize that Americans practiced widespread slavery), fewer people understand the horrors that Black people in America faced shortly after the close of America's peculiar institution. The decisions made by people in power during this period ensured that White supremacy would be imbedded into the foundation of modern America.

The 13th Amendment to the United States Constitution officially ended slavery in 1865. Over the next few years, legislators passed a series of laws that transitioned enslaved Black people from owned property to humans and citizens of the United States. This era became known as Reconstruction and was a fleeting moment where it looked like America was veering toward full racial equality.

11

The Civil Rights Act of 1866 "declared that all persons born in the United States, except untaxed Indians, were citizens of the United States and as such were entitled to equality of treatment before the law..." (Logan, 1965, p. 20). In the same year, the 14th Amendment to the Constitution was proposed, which further buttressed Black people's claims to citizenship and equal rights. Section 1 of the 14th Amendment states:

> All persons born or naturalized in the United States and subject to the jurisdiction thereof, are citizens of the United States and of the state in wherein they reside. No state shall make or enforce any law which shall abridge the privileges or immunities of the citizens of the United States; nor shall any state deprive any person of life, liberty, or property, without due process of law; nor deny to any person within its jurisdiction the equal protection of the laws.

The federal government aggressively pushed through the new civil rights legislation, partially as a response to Black people's needs and, in part, to punish the South for its role in the Civil War. As a part of the Reconstruction Act of 1867, each of the states that formerly made up the Confederacy had to agree to ratify the 14th Amendment to regain admission to the Union (Anderson, 1992).

The Civil Rights Act of 1866 and the 14th Amendment protected many Black people's rights but did not guarantee them the right to vote, but the 15th Amendment soon addressed that issue. Ratified in 1870, the 15th Amendment gave male citizens the right to vote regardless of their race or previous servitude condition. Five years later, the Civil Rights Act of 1875 was passed, which outlawed discrimination against Black people in public places and public carriers (Logan, 1965). For the first time, in very concrete terms, Black people had legal guarantees of their rights and position in America. Moreover, to ensure that the South was making good on its promise to follow the new laws, the federal government placed troops in the South to protect Black people and their newly won rights.

In addition to all of the Reconstruction era's civil rights legislation mentioned above, the federal government also established what became known as the "Freedmen's Bureau." The Freedmen's Bureau was responsible for helping Black people adjust from slavery to freedom. The Freedmen's Bureau provided tremendous relief for many Black people who started their journey into freedom with nothing but the ragged clothes on their backs. John Hope Franklin wrote:

> Between 1865 and 1869, for example, the bureau issued 21 million rations, approximately 5 million going to whites and 15 million going to blacks, By 1867 there were forty-six hospitals...The medical department spent over $2 million to improve the health of exslaves and treated more than 450,000 cases of illness. The death rate among former slaves was reduced, and sanitary conditions were improved (1994, p. 229).

The Freedmen's Bureau also helped newly freed Black people find homes, secure labor, and even be transported to less congested areas where they could become self-supporting (Franklin, 1994). Franklin wrote that the Bureau's most outstanding achievement was providing educational opportunities for Black people. The Bureau arranged schools ranging from Sunday schools to industrial schools to colleges. Several of the Black colleges that exist today (e.g., Howard University, Hampton University, and Fisk University) received financial assistance from the

Bureau. By the time the Bureau finished its educational work, they had been responsible for educating 247,333 students in 4,239 schools (Franklin, 1994).

The Reconstruction era provided a new world of opportunity in politics as well. Now that Black men had the right to vote, they were a potent electoral force, particularly in areas where they comprised the majority of the population. The Reconstruction era is responsible for a list of firsts for Black people in politics. P.B.S. Pinchback of Louisiana became the first Black Governor in the United States in 1873, which was a feat that would not be repeated until 1989 when Douglass Wilder won the Virginia gubernatorial race. John Roy Lynch became the first Black to hold the title of Mississippi's Speaker of the House in 1872. Jonathan Jasper Wright became the first Black to be elected to the Pennsylvania Bar and the first Black to serve on South Carolina's Supreme Court (Franklin, 1994).

For the first time, it looked like America was making good on its promise of "liberty and justice for all." Unfortunately, this was not to be the case for very long. In a pattern that would frequently repeat itself in American history, just as Black people were beginning to feel that they were getting what they deserved, White people began to think that they already had too much. Black people were about to come out of their dream of a fair and equal America and wake into a reality that was an absolute nightmare.

Even while Black people were beginning to grow accustomed to the taste of freedom, White people in the South actively worked to put limits on that freedom. Shortly after Congress ratified the 13th Amendment, Southern states rolled out the "Black Codes" (Logan, 1965). The Black Codes were the Southern states' attempt to maintain control over Black people, even without the institution of slavery. They resembled the slave codes that governed the movement and legal behavior of slaves before emancipation and included some new tricks. Vagrancy, which the state essentially defined as not working for a White person, was outlawed. Vagrancy laws forced Black people to take jobs with employers that would abuse them, knowing that they could not quit for fear of being imprisoned (Franklin, 1994).

Even after the 14th and 15th Amendments were ratified, Southern Whites continued to fight to preserve the way of life they had grown accustomed to. During Reconstruction, Southern Whites painted a portrait of Black people as dangerous animals on the loose. Southern Whites perceived Black people's newfound freedom and growing power as an invasion that they needed to fend off. To this end, White people in the South became determined to establish "home rule," which resulted in Black people becoming the victims of uncountable acts of terror. The desire to restore White supremacy to full strength in the South led to the rise of a wave of White terrorist groups, including the White Brotherhood, the Pale Faces, the Rifle Clubs of South Carolina, and the most influential group, the Ku Klux Klan (Logan, 1965). These groups and like-minded individual citizens unleashed a wave of terror on Black people that would last for nearly one hundred years. Rayford Logan described the worse decades of this period as the "nadir," meaning the lowest point in race relations.

The Compromise of 1877 was the key event that explains how Black people went from having more power and rights than they had ever previously enjoyed to being reduced to a state that, in some cases, was worse than slavery. In the Presidential election of 1876, the Republican candidate, Rutherford B. Hayes, won the electoral vote but lost the popular vote to the Democratic candidate, Samuel Tilden. There was also a dispute over 20 of the electoral votes. A Republican-led commission was appointed to investigate the matter. They determined that Hayes was the rightful winner, but the commission's findings were not final until the House of Representatives, which the Democrats controlled, approved it. To sway Congress toward accepting his legitimacy as President, Hayes gave the Democrats three concessions:

1. Hayes would remove federal troops from the South.

2. The federal government would pay for improvements in rail and waterway transportation in the South.

3. Hayes would appoint a conservative Southerner to his cabinet (Danzer, 2002).

With the removal of federal troops from the South and the end of Reconstruction, the South instituted a revamped version of the Black Codes to ensure that Black people would stay in their assigned place firmly beneath White people. This system was nicknamed "Jim Crow." Jim Crow was a collection of laws and customs that attempted to control every aspect of Black life from the most monumental action to the most minute. These White supremacist laws across America forced Black people to operate under laws that were awesome in their thoroughness. Leon Litwack in, *Trouble in Mind* (1998), gives numerous examples that show the oppressive environment White people in the Jim Crow South forced Black people to live in:

- Black people were segregated from White people on all means of public transportation. As such, Black people had to sit in segregated waiting rooms, and once on a train, were forced to sit in second-class or smoking cars. Some cities also found it necessary to pay for separate streetcars to reduce the chance of a White person having any more contact with a Black person than absolutely necessary. (pp. 231, 232) .

- Black people were not allowed in the same hotels or restaurants as White people, as their very presence would evoke feelings of disgust in them (p. 231).

- Black people were not allowed to try on clothes at department stores (p. 233).

- If Black people were allowed to go to the same movie theaters as White people, they were sometimes required to buy their tickets from a separate box office, enter through a separate entrance, and sit in the balcony (p. 233).

- Black motorists were not allowed to pass White motorists on unpaved or dusty roads for fear that White motorists would take it as a sign of impudence or worst yet, they would splash dirt or mud on them (p. 235).

- Black and White children were not to share the same textbooks.

- Courts would not allow Black people to be sworn in on the same Bible as White people.

- Black people had separate telephone booths, separate windows for banks, and even separate elevators in some cases.

- Some cities went as far as to separate Black and White prostitutes to prevent them from working in the same areas.

- Black people were not permitted to live in the same neighborhoods as White people.
- Jim Crow even extended into death as Black people were not allowed to be buried in the same cemeteries, and White people sometimes wondered how God could tolerate niggers in heaven) (p. 236).
- Black people were not allowed to vote.
- The greatest crime was sexual contact between Black men and White women.

The examples of Jim Crow laws above serve as only a small example of the detailed list of racial rules Black people were forced to follow, not only in the South but also in much of the North. Black people's failure to quickly learn how to navigate this minefield of racism, discrimination, and violence, could easily mean death because of the wrong gesture, word, or look.

The punishment of choice was lynching. The word "lynch' means to put to death by mob action without legal sanction or due process of law. As it applied to Black people, lynching was also a means by which White people intimidated Black people into submissive behavior. During the nadir, lynchings were recurrent throughout both the North and South. In *A Rage for Order*, Joel Williamson explains that by the 1890s, there was a definite pattern to lynchings. Lynchings usually occurred in places where they had happened before, in places where murders and rapists had been able to escape punishment, and in areas where there was economic uncertainty. White anxiety over real crime aside, White people showed a consistent tendency to lynch Black people for almost any crime they even thought they might have committed. White people did not intend for Black people to see lynchings as an act against an

When a lynching occurred, it did not matter if a lynch mob found the crime's actual perpetrator. As long as White people punished any Black person, they accomplished their mission.

individual but rather the whole Black race. When Black people refused to follow the demeaning customs of Jim Crow, White people viewed it as a sign that the entire race was becoming too uppity and needed a reminder of where their place was. Thus, when a lynching occurred, it did not matter if a lynch mob found the crime's actual perpetrator. As long as White people punished any Black person, they accomplished their mission (Williamson, 1986).

Unfortunately, there is no shortage of stories of the horrors of lynchings. Ralph Ginzburg published a collection of newspaper clips on lynchings entitled, *100 Years of Lynching in America*, that revealed an astonishing lack of recognition of the humanity of Black people in America. The lynchings that Black people fell victim to varied in their cruelty. In September of 1912, a lynch mob killed a Black man in Princeton, West Virginia, when they mistakenly thought he attacked a 14 year-old White girl. After the mob executed the man, the mayor admitted that he did not come close to fitting the description of the actual rape suspect (Ginzburg, 1988).

In Louisiana, in 1913, a Black man by the name of Watkins Lewis suffered viciously at the hands of another lynch mob:

> Stories here tonight tell of a mob of 200 white men, formed in the outskirts of Sylvester last night. Lewis, cringing with fear, was taken from the jail here, placed in a motor car, and

19

whirled to the mob. Not a word was spoken as the little cavalcade formed, and with the Negro in the center marched to a giant tree near the Texas line, Lewis was bound to the trunk.

Fallen trees and branches were heaped about him. Before the fire was lighted Lewis repeatedly was asked to confess his part in the crime, or to divulge the hiding place for a large sum of money said to have been stolen from the postmaster's store. "I didn't do it," he screamed as the flames leaped about him (Ginzburg, 1988, p. 93).

Women were no safer from White lynch mobs than men were. One of the most horrific incidents of "mob justice" came at the expense of a Black woman in Georgia. Mary Turner was an eight-month pregnant Black woman whose husband was lynched and vowed revenge on those who had killed him. As a result, a mob of several hundred White men gathered and captured Turner. The mob then proceeded to tie her ankles together and hang her upside down. They then doused her clothes with gasoline and set them afire. After her clothes burned from her body, a member of the mob slit her stomach open with a knife and let her premature baby fall to the ground. Someone from the mob then crushed the baby with the heel of his shoe, after which the mob finally killed Turner by firing hundreds of bullets into her body (Litwack, 1998).

Unfortunately, the savagery of Turner's murder was not uncommon. Lynchings were public events, not secret rituals. They were often events that entire families attended for entertainment. There are numerous photographs of White people smiling as they posed with corpses of hanged and torched Black bodies. In some cases, Black victims

20

were mutilated and had their fingers, ears, and other pieces of flesh passed out to the crowds of onlookers as souvenirs (Litwack, 1998).

What made lynchings even more terrifying for Black people was the randomness of those chosen for execution (Marable, 1983). Lynch mobs did not always put much effort into finding the actual Black person who they thought committed a wrong. Since the purpose of lynching was to send a message to the Black community, it did not really matter which Black person White vigilantes punished. As long as the Black community got the message to stay in their place, it did not really matter which "nigger" died. Manning Marable in *How Capitalism Underdeveloped Black America*, wrote that "[t]error is not the product of violence alone, but is created only by the random, senseless and even bestial use of coercion against an entire population" (1983, 118). Between 1896 and 1946, lynch mobs murdered almost 4,000 Black people, but the effect of those killings spread to everyone in the Black community (Williamson, 1986). Facing each day, not knowing whether their wife, husband, child or themselves, would be the next burnt corpse found in the woods was a daily reality for the entire Black community.

White people, of course, expected Black people to stay silent about the unjust murders of their families and neighbors and to accept the rationale that White people were only protecting their communities from dangerous Black creatures. Black people who dared to complain were met with fierce resistance from their White neighbors. The famed protector of Black people's civil rights, Ida B. Wells-Barnett, exposed lynchings for what they really were through her writings. In her writings, Wells-Barnett argued that White people's fear of Black rapists was an excuse to

21

cover up lynchings' real purpose, which was to force Black people into an inferior position under White people. As result of her campaign against lynching, Ida B. Wells-Barnett received several serious death threats that forced her to flee the South and go into hiding (Gilmore, 1996).

The reward for those Black people that were able to survive during the nadir was daily humiliation. A collection of scholars combined their efforts to produce a volume entitled, *Remembering Jim Crow*, which contains numerous first-person accounts of the trials of living through the Jim Crow era. Ann Pointer recalled having to walk past several closer "White" schools on her way to the school designated for Black children. Pointer had to walk to school because Black people could not use the school busses even though Black residents' tax dollars helped pay for them. Pointer recalled, "Nothing rode the busses but the whites. And they would ride and throw trash, throw rocks and everything at us on the road and hoop and holler, 'nigger, nigger, nigger,' all up and down the road" (qtd. in Chafe, 2001, p. 155).

As White people were discriminating against Black children in schools, they were also discriminating against Black adults at the polls. The 15th Amendment should have ensured that at least Black men would be able to participate in elections. But Black voters were soon to find out that laws are meaningless words if no one is willing to enforce them. White people disfranchised Black people in several ways. One such way was literacy tests in which poorly educated Black people would have to read and understand complicated materials that most White people were not able to comprehend (Packard, p. 68). White people used the slightest mistake by Black people on the test as an excuse to not allow them to vote. In addition to literacy tests, the grandfather clause barred Black people whose grandparents had not previously voted from voting in current elections. The grandfather clause was particularly troubling for Black people in the South during this period as most of their grandparents were slaves who, of course, could not vote. In other cases, White people required potential Black voters to pay for the right to vote. By establishing a poll tax, even if it was a small fee, White people knew it would be enough to prevent many Black people from voting. Even if Black people met all the qualifications to vote, White people still had the luxury of forgetting to submit their names as registered voters on Election Day (Packard, 2002, p. 67).

What is most disturbing is that states considered these tactics legal. Southern states rewrote their constitutions to include laws that would disfranchise Black people. The federal government accepted the argument that electoral processes were a matter for the states to handle. The damage to Black people's political power was drastic. For instance, Louisiana went from having 130,000 registered Black voters before the state adopted a new constitution that made Black people have to jump through a series of hoops to vote to only 5,000 registered Black voters afterward (Packard, 2002, pp. 68, 69).

Underneath all of the special controls put on Black life was White people's uncertainty of Black people's humanity. White people saw Black men, in particular, as threats to Southern society. They viewed them as the antithesis of Southern White women. While Southern women were supposed to be beautiful, innocent, and virtuous, Black men were seen as hideous, criminal, super-sexual beasts. Some White people went as far as to argue that Black people' natural state was that of an animal. Slavery and Jim Crow laws were necessary to keep, or at least slow down,

Black people's retrogression into their natural state of bestiality (Williamson, 1986). The 1905 novel, *The Clansman*, which was later turned into the first blockbuster film, *Birth of a Nation*, highlighted this belief. *Birth of a Nation* is a fictitious account of life in the South after the Civil War. The movie presented Black men as sex-craved animals who split their days between raping White women and destroying the South's political system. The movie concludes with White people erecting the Ku Klux Klan to rescue the South and restore order by putting Black people back into subservient roles. *Birth of Nation* was wildly successful and even received a favorable review in the White House by President Woodrow Wilson.

Shortly after the publication of the Clansman, an event unfolded in the North that showed just how animal-like White people thought Black people were. In 1904, a group of White men traveled to Africa and captured several Efe men. The Black men were brought back to America and displayed in a cage at the World's Fair in St. Louis. In 1906, after the fair's conclusion, one of the Black men, Ota Benga, was put in a monkey cage for display at the Bronx Zoo in New York. The idea that White people could kidnap Black people and permanently imprison them in a zoo sent shockwaves of terror through the Black community. The ordeal was too much for Ota Benga to handle, as well, as he eventually took his own life at the age of 28 (Evanzz, 1999, pp. 2425).

To counteract the notion that they were uncivilized animals, some Black people made special efforts to show White people just how "civilized" they could be. A number of Black people tried to negotiate a compromise in which White people would allow those Black people who behaved in the same manner as middle-class White people, the

24

privileges of voting and holding political offices (Gilmore, 1996, p. 62). Famed educator Booker T. Washington encouraged Black people to conform to White middle-class standards and stay in the South and prove that they were as sophisticated, civilized, and hardworking as White people. The problem, though, was that when Black people showed how successful they could be, White people often met them with tremendous violence. In a pattern that would be repeated throughout the country, White people assaulted thriving Black communities. Race riots broke out in Atlanta, New Orleans, Tulsa, and Wilmington, to name a few of the cities where White people attacked Black communities. James Weldon Johnson referred to the summer of 1919 as the "Red Summer" because of all of the blood shed in race riots that season.

Black people tried to show that they were as upright, hardworking, and civilized as White people to gain their acceptance, but when they succeeded, White people despised them instead of embracing them. Joel Williamson beautifully summed up Black people's predicament in the following passage about the race riot in Atlanta:

> The great mass of blacks in Atlanta had been doing precisely what whites told them to do working, churching, and quietly managing their own affairs. They had been doing what Booker T. Washington had advised all blacks to do...more than a decade before. They had cast down their buckets where they were, and now the water came up salty, bitter, and foul (1986, p. 149).

There seemed to be no end to the injustices to which Black people were exposed. Everything Black people did seem to be a crime worthy of death or other severe punishment. One of the severe forms of punishment that

White people subjected Black people to was the prison farm system they developed in the South during this period. In, *Worse than Slavery*," David Oshinsky examines how, during the nadir, various states in the South adopted convict leasing systems that allowed businesspeople to rent workers from prisons. As a result, elected officials passed new laws that allowed Black people to be arrested, convicted, and sentenced to ridiculous terms so that Southern states could profit off their prison labor. For instance, in Alabama, the number of Black people arrested and convicted depended on the coal companies' need for workers. When the coal companies needed more workers, the police would hit the streets and arrest hundreds of Black people for crimes as small as drunkenness or vagrancy, convict them, and sentence them to two to three months of hard labor. Once convicted, they were led to the coal mines to work off their crimes, and by nightfall, they would be working twelve to sixteen-hour shifts (Oshinsky, 1996, p. 77).

What makes the story of Black people in America unique is that the discrimination and abuse they experienced happened within the context of the law. Over many generations, millions of Black people gave their all to America, and in return, the country legalized White people's treatment of them as subhumans. From the Dred Scott decision, in which the court ruled that enslaved Black people were a lesser class of beings that "had no rights which

What makes the story of Black people in America unique is that the discrimination and abuse they experienced happened within the context of the law.

a White man was bound to respect," to Plessy v. Ferguson in which the Supreme Court ruled that segregation was legal, to the Jim Crow laws, the United States made clear that Black people were unwelcome as equal partners in the American dream.

The codification of racism towards Black people was a particularly hard pill to swallow as they watched White immigrants come to America and receive better treatment than they did. One example of this was the settlement house movement. Settlement houses were places of transition where newly arrived immigrants could live and be taught the skills necessary to function in America successfully. Aid from settlement houses was a courtesy White people denied many Black people as they moved from the rural South to the urban North, which was equivalent to moving to a new country for many Black people. As more Black people moved to the cities, settlement houses chose to move rather than help them (Lasch-Quinn, 1993, p. 25). The settlement housing movement's spurring of Black Americans added insult to injury as Black people who served the country faithfully for centuries were passed over for people who had never previously touched American soil.

Another problem Black people faced as they moved into America's cities was housing discrimination. Again in a completely legal move, White people created restrictive covenant agreements that prevented Black people from moving into specific neighborhoods. A restrictive covenant is a contract that excludes specific ethnic groups from purchasing a property. When a person buys a property with a restrictive covenant on it, they agree to not sell the property to people the covenant prohibits. Some covenants went so far as to even limit the number of Black people that could work in a home. The covenants' signers paid a fee, had the agreement notarized to make it binding, and then filed it at city hall, or they had the covenant written into the real estate deed for the property (Stewart, 1996). The effect was the creation of covenant blocks that could legally exclude Black people from residing there.

The few examples that I mentioned in this chapter are only a small sampling of the kinds of oppression Black people endured during the century between emancipation and the civil rights movement of the 1950s and 1960s. Everyday, Black Americans' White neighbors forced them to live in a world that seemed to despise them no matter what they did. James Weldon Johnson profoundly described this era of Black life in, *Lift Every Voice and Sing,* when he wrote:

> *We have come over a way that with tears has been watered.*
>
> *We have come treading our path through the blood of the slaughtered.*

There are no words to accurately describe the pain Black people felt living in an era where it was a crime to be both Black and alive. It is in the context of this incredibly volatile world that Black children, en masse, tried to get a formal education for the first time. Entrusting the social, emotional, and intellectual well-being of Black children to the ideas of White educators and politicians during this period was like trusting lions to care for a herd of antelopes. Predictably, Black schools faced incredible challenges that are still with us today.

Lesson 5: The Identity Crisis of Black Schools

G iven the century of trauma that we examined in the previous lesson, one can imagine how difficult it was to establish schools that could effectively educate Black children. Because they faced unique problems, Black people also needed an education uniquely designed to create solutions to those problems. In the context of the violently racist world in which they lived, a number of educators championed competing educational philosophies that they believed would enable Black people to survive and excel in America.

Often educators were divided into two schools of thought on how to educate Black people best. One camp promoted a classical education while the other supported an industrial-centered education. However, Carter G. Woodson believed that both the classical education that Black people were receiving at colleges and the industrial training proposed by Black leaders like Booker T. Washington were both woefully inadequate to meet Black people's real-life needs. Woodson concluded that there was no advantage to Black people going to college if they were not going to learn information that would allow them to help solve Black people's unique problems. He argued that having more college-educated Black people becomes a disadvantage if colleges are training them to fit in and to support the same racist system that caused Black people's problems in the first place. About Black colleges, for instance, Woodson writes:

> If these institutions are to be the replica of Harvard, Yale, Columbia, and Chicago, if the

men that administer them and teach are to be the products of rolltop desk theorists who have never touched the life of the Negro, the money thus invested will be just as profitably spent if it's used to buy peanuts to throw at animals in a circus (2000, p. 31).

Once at school, Black people were often subjected to an education that held them back instead of advancing. Woodson examined the psychological damage that many schools put Black people through in *The MisEducation of the Negro*. As mentioned previously, Black people in slavery had been conditioned by White people to believe that they had no history of which to speak. This trend continued in many of the schools Black people attended after emancipation. Woodson believed that the elimination of Black people's history ensured that White people would always hold a superior position over them. If White people could make Black people accept the story that their people had always been failures, Black people would have little reason to expect anything other than continual failure for themselves. This was a powerful weapon whose essence Woodson sums up in his famous quote:

When you control a man's thinking you do not have to worry about his actions. You do not have to tell him not to stand here or go yonder. He will find his 'proper place' and will stay in it. You do not need to send him to the back door. He will go without being told. In fact, if there is no back door, he will cut one for his special benefit. His education makes it necessary (Woodson, 2000, p. xix).

In 1933, Woodson recognized the most significant barrier to Black people receiving a meaningful and empowering education in America–White supremacy. Today, schools still have not entirely eliminated White supremacist assumptions from the curriculum that Black children ingest. While a White supremacist education can take the form of directly insulting and questioning the value and necessity of Black life, it more frequently manifests itself by ignoring Black people and not recognizing their unique historical experience in America. Without schools recognizing that Black students need an education that empowers them to address and solve the problems and challenges that face their particular communities, schools are only miseducating them. Woodson asserts that a real education for Black students requires that they simply be taught to deal with conditions as they are in the Black community instead of how we would like or wish them to be (Woodson, 2000, p. xvii).

In, *Miseducation to Education*, psychologist, Na'im Akbar, explains the difference between being educated and being trained:

> ...education is a process by which you are more actively capable of manifesting what you are. When you increasingly manifest what somebody else wants you to be which may or may not be critical to your survival as a life form you are actually trained (1982, p. 3).

One of Black students' central problems is that their schools force them to learn in an environment that is still replete with White supremacy's history and influence. Even school districts controlled by predominately Black school boards and administrators too often fail to address this problem. This lack of educational innovation is not surprising because White supremacist laced school systems trained these Black school leaders and taught them to perpetuate the same oppressive system that has always been in existence (Pitre & Pitre, 2008). Thus, they continue the practice of training Black students rather than educating them.

Schools are not preparing Black students to challenge the White power structure that exists in American society today. Creating Black thinkers that are committed to upending the racism and inequality of American society is not at the core of most Black students' curriculum. In urban schools that are often populated by Black children, there is usually more emphasis placed on standardized test scores than on creating young people capable of meeting their world's unique challenges.

Black students' schools train them to find their place in the White power structure as it currently exists. In my travels as a teacher, most of my students tell me that they are going to college because it will lead to them landing a good job. Black people are often patted on the back when they say that they want to work for a big corporation, but Black children's schools should be emphasizing the expansion of Black ownership rather than Black labor. Regardless of the field they want to enter, educators should be teaching Black students to be employers, not employees. Nevertheless, this idea seems foreign to many of the Black students with which I have worked. They are simply content to work for White people.

Many Black youths have this mentality because their schools do an abysmal job teaching Black youth their history and culture. By concentrating so heavily on the historical contributions of White historical figures and events in Social Studies classes, and the works of White writers in their English classes, schools have sent the same message that slave masters sent to their enslaved Africans: Your history and culture are insignificant and, consequently, so are you. The only people worth studying are people of European descent. Everyone else is just tangential to humanity's main story, which is that of White people.

In the 21st century, neither the physical enslavement of Black Americans nor Jim Crow Laws are necessary to deny Black people opportunities for advancement, self-dignity, or recognition as full human beings. The schools that Black students attend all but ensure that they will grow up to be almost entirely powerless people. There is no longer a need to have a complicated system of laws or White overseers to stand watch over Black people to make sure that they do not rise above their condition of servitude. Every day, our schools thoroughly train Black students to be obedient servants and defenders of the social, political, and cultural order as it currently exists.

White supremacy wrecks havoc on Black students' psyche who are forced to endure years of miseducation. In the next lesson, we will examine precisely how schools' refusal to recognize and remove White supremacy's influence on Black students' schools creates a host of problems in the Black community.

Lesson 6: The Psychological Necessity of Black History

The effect of Black students being trained instead of educated is very clear in today's schools. There is a desperate need for the schools that teach Black children to develop curriculum and instructional strategies that can serve as an effective countermeasure against the onslaught of negative images that dominant White America fires at Black youth. As a result of being subjected to school systems that continually dismiss Black students' specific needs, Black students have developed attitudes and behaviors that are self-destructive. There are any number of glaring problems that are devastating schools with predominately Black student populations. In my travels as a teacher and lecturer, I consistently encounter Black students that suffer from various combinations of the following problems:

- Low self-esteem
- Rampant feeling of powerlessness
- Widespread incidents of self-hate
- Low expectations for personal achievement
- Low expectations for group achievement
- Inability to critically examine society
- Passive acceptance of White supremacist ideas
- No understanding of the importance of history in their daily lives
- Difficulty supporting arguments with factual historical information
- An under-appreciation of the privileges that they have and the sacrifices made to secure them

35

All of the above problems are predictable in a Black population whose schools have exposed them to almost no history of themselves. The possession of various combinations of these problems by many Black students results in them feeling utterly powerless. They can perceive that their society is shortchanging them in many ways but feel that they can do nothing about it. They perceive themselves as pawns in a larger game over which they have no control. Black youth want to avoid this feeling of powerlessness and connect to something important, but Black communities suffer from a paucity of meaningful and powerful youth outlets. As such, gangs sometimes serve as a source of power for young Black youth as membership instantaneously makes one a part of something bigger and stronger than what they were as individuals. Reformed Los Angeles gang member, Kody "Monster" Scott, wrote:

> If I had been born in '53 instead of '63, I would have been a Black Panther. If I had been born in Germany in the early '30s I would probably have joined the Nationalist Socialist Party. If I had been born Jewish, I would have joined the Jewish Defense League because I have the energy, the vitality, to be part of something with power, either constructive or destructive. And because there was a destructive element around me growing up, I went into the Crips (qtd. in Kunjufu 1995, p. 167).

Herein lies the importance of history and African and African American Studies to young Black students. Black youth want to feel connected to something powerful. However, they do not realize that their history automatically connects them to some of the greatest and most powerful people to have ever walked the planet.

The social sciences are not objective or passive entities. History, for instance, is a tool that provides several active functions. Psychologist, Amos Wilson, asserted that "people who manipulate the past and present manipulate one's mentality, sanity, contact with reality and the ability to deal with reality" (Wilson, 1993, p. 43). History creates a shared identity of a people. Without a shared identity, there is no basis for a group to collectively act to improve their lives (Wilson, 1993). Since most of my students have almost no historical knowledge of Africans throughout the Diaspora, they feel no connection to anything larger than themselves. Thus, they

"People who manipulate the past and present manipulate one's mentality, sanity, contact with reality and the ability to deal with reality."

tend to distance themselves instead of uniting with Black people in the United States or abroad to resist oppression because they have internalized White supremacists' perception of Black people as inferior. Without knowing their own history, they cannot counter the negative images that the larger dominant White society thrusts at them that weakens their collective power.

Black History can also be viewed as a geometrical concept in that it locates and positions one relative to the rest of the world (Wilson, 1993). Without an understanding of one's own history, one cannot be conscious as Na'im Akbar defines it:

> Consciousness is awareness... Awareness is the ability to see accurately what is. Being able to see accurately means that one must be properly oriented in space, time, and person,

which means that the prerequisite for consciousness is to have some accurate image of one's self and the world in which one finds himself (Akbar, 1993, p. 12).

When one loses consciousness, they cannot view the world rationally; their perception of the world is distorted and leads to behavior inconsistent with their own or their community's self-interest. Colton Simpson, a former Crip gang member in Los Angeles, recalled a clear example of how losing one's consciousness could make a person act in insane ways. In prison, Simpson had a conversation with another gang member who explained that he learned the techniques they used to break in new cellmates from reading a book on how slaves were "broken" when they first came to a plantation. He explained:

> "You gotta read this book. It tells all about what the slave master did to us...The first thing you do is make the slave feel your power, your control." He zips up his pants and places his hands on his waist. "Then you degrade him. That's why you jerk his shorts in his ass. He feels like a bitch then. Less than man. Wit' threats and shows of aggression fool ready to do anything...Then you tie his ass up to let him know you the master" (Simpson & Pearlman, 2005, p. 195).

As Simpson thought about the conversation he just had, he realized that he was witnessing a psychological need to be viewed as powerful:

> This is how it must feel to have absolute power, to do with another as we wish. Humiliate him, sexually abuse him, torture him, watch all the pride ebb away. Each pleading, each sorrowful abased look and moan, increases our sense of authority, strength, invulnerability. And yes,

he hardly seemed human...The slave book was brought in to teach us Crips history, but we turned it around and started doing what the white guys did to us. Instead of, "Do unto others as you'd do unto you," we do unto others as has been done to us (Simpson & Pearlman, 2005, pp. 195, 197).

Simpson's conclusion is the premise of Amos Wilson's classic study on so-called Black-on-Black Violence. Wilson contends that the violence that we see perpetrated in the Black community is the manifestation of Black people's exposure to centuries of their White oppressors' tactics to gain power and control over their environments. Black criminals actually internalized the lessons that White America has taught them and put them into action. Wilson explains that while mainstream society does not perceive them as criminals, it is, in fact, the White middle and ruling classes that dominate crime:

> Their apparent non-criminality is mainly due to the fact that they define what crime is, and define out of existence their own crimes. Their criminal activities are delegated through their police forces (enforcers), armed forces (gangs), bankers (loan sharks), salespersons and advertising agents (con artists), businessmen (extortionists making offers others cannot refuse), diplomats (frontmen), corporations (rackets), consortiums (drugs and other types of rings), and numerous other euphemistically named organizations whose nefarious activities are whitewashed...and legitimized by their power. Their taking of property, wealth, dignity, and lives of others by force is called war; their major massacres are called World War I and World War II... (Wilson, 1990, pp. 9091).

Wilson goes further and argues that White America demands that Black criminality exists to fulfill their psychological needs. Wilson states that White people "...need to projectively perceive the African male as criminal, to psychosocially and politico-economically condition his criminality, is reflective of repressed White American guilt and criminality" (Wilson, 1990, p. 2). In other words, White Americans must distort reality in order to enjoy their spoils of war without feeling guilty. Because White America has been guilty of so much crime (e.g., the maltreatment and destruction of nations, the murder and exploitation of native peoples and their lands, the denial of the humanity of non-White people across the globe, chattel slavery, lynching, etc.), they need to convince themselves that Black people somehow deserved whatever White people have done to them. Thus, White people's perception of Black people as evil and criminal allows them to rationalize their criminal behavior without feeling guilty. (Wilson, 1990).

The distortion and suppression of Black history by those in power in America is not an accident. Europeans have consistently used the distortion of history as a tool to weaken the populations they sought to rule. Others more easily manipulate people who have no sense of history because they have no basis for understanding different people's motivations and psychology (Wilson, 1993). By not having control over or even access to their own history, Black students often cannot ground themselves, see the world clearly from their own point of view, and act in their own self-interest.

Intentionally or not, when schools teach Black students to view themselves from their oppressor's point of view, Black students become conditioned to believe that the

White ruling class's behavior is normal when some psychologists argue their behavior is narcissistic. Narcissism means extreme selfishness, with a grandiose view of one's own talents and a craving for admiration. A person or group that is narcissistic possesses an inflated ego that makes them believe that they are the world's center. For the narcissist, having the desire to want something is justification enough to get it by any means. The only rights they accord others are those that the narcissist allows them to have. Because their ego is so inflated, it distorts their view of the world to make it seem like all of their actions, no matter how immoral, are justified and necessary (Karenga, 1993). Because schools condition Black students to see much of what White people do as normal, Black youth are rarely critical of America's White power structure and will never seek to change it.

The low self-esteem and low expectations that many Black students possess, and the distorted sense of awe they feel towards White people's power and accomplishments, are predictable considering their lack of knowledge of their own history.

Perceptual psychologists argue that the best guarantee that a person will effectively deal with the future is that person experiencing success in their past (Oliva, 2005). It is difficult for Black students to develop a positive self-concept when they have no information to counterbalance the onslaught of negative images and stereotypes that White society thrusts upon them in their daily lives. "It is necessary to provide experiences that teach the individuals they are positive people" (Oliva 2005, p. 169). Black history provides just such an experience for Black students.

Sometimes Black students find various ways to compensate for their lack of confidence and self-esteem that the knowledge of their history would provide. Amos Wilson points out that Black Americans do this by adorning themselves in the latest fashions and luxury items in some cases. Instead of viewing their bodies as living, breathing, human flesh, the body becomes an object whose purpose is to display flashy items. The body ceases to be human and merely becomes a mannequin or (more accurately) a dummy to display as many material items as possible. Black people see the mannequin with the most and flashiest items on it as the best and most admirable one (Wilson, 1990). This is the attitude that many Black students exhibit as they grow dependent on external entities to provide them with a sense of self-worth.

Black youths' materialism is the predictable outgrowth of an entire culture obsessed with gathering material goods. This problem is particularly rampant in the Black community, where Black people have become consistent consumers of products and almost nonexistent producers. Black America's lack of historical purpose and cohesiveness has led to a state of mental slavery where they hold on to practices and beliefs that slavers instilled into their ancestors during the seasoning process we examined previously.

In 2005, the CBS television program, Dr. Phil, provided a perfect example of this miseducated mind at work. The theme of the show was people who spend money beyond their means. The first guests on the show were a Black couple who wasted incredible amounts of money on designer clothes and luxury cars that they could not afford. The couple could not afford to both pay their monthly utility bills on time and maintain their wealthy appearance, so they intentionally did not pay their utility bills until they got shut off notices. At that point, they only paid just enough of their bills to keep their utilities on, while continuing to spend the rest of their money on more luxury items that they could not afford. The couple continued to do this even after they were forced to declare bankruptcy and lost their first home to creditors. The couple also had three children for whom they had no college savings plan in place.

The couple's commitment to looking like they were rich and powerful was ridiculously strong. For example, they owned a Lexus that needed repairs that they could not afford. The husband took out a $13,000 loan to pay for the car repairs but instead used the money to buy himself a new motorcycle that he almost immediately crashed. Then instead of finding a way to get their current car fixed, they took out another auto loan to purchase an SUV whose monthly payment they could not afford (Tobin, 2005).

After explaining the couple's situation to his studio audience, Dr. Phil, asked a question whose answer was obvious to me. He asked the couple why they continue to spend money that they clearly do not have. Their predictable response was that they did not want White people to perceive them as just another poor Black family. Here is a miseducated mind in perfect action: Instead of having a mindset focused on providing the best possible future for their family, this couple decides to almost ruin their lives and the lives of their children, in the hope of being respected by White people. I can only imagine that it broke that couple's heart when Dr. Phil calmly explained to them that he, nor anyone else, was impressed with what they had. The way this couple managed their finances actually had just the opposite effect of what they wanted. The mostly White audience had looks of disgust on their faces as they watched how this couple lived. The miseducated Black person is obsessed with earning their master's respect, but their master usually does not know they exist. If he does, he could care less about whatever trinkets of wealth they flash.

Sadly, this couple is not exceptional in the Black community. While teaching, I often encounter examples of this obsession to impress others with flashy material goods to compensate for a lack of self-respect, pride, and sense of importance. I worked in high schools where hundreds of poor kids spent four years trying to pass themselves off as wealthy. Some kids lived in the projects but wore belts that cost hundreds of dollars and owned multiple pairs of sneakers that cost nearly $200 each. I have also observed Black people in economically depressed neighborhoods that can find a way to own (at least for a while) luxury cars but cannot find a way to move their children to a better neighborhood. Miseducated people are focused on the symbols of success instead of the substance of success.

Miseducated people are focused on the symbols of success instead of the substance of success.

This phenomenon occurs when Black people are still operating under miseducation. Many Black people are completely consumed with looking like they are successful, which they hope will in turn, gain them the respect from White people that they subconsciously admire so much. One of the disturbing habits of miseducated people is their inability to put their own family's needs ahead of their obsession to gain acceptance from White people.

Part of Black America's problem is the same problem that almost all Americans, regardless of race, suffer from: Americans are obsessed with collecting material goods.

Americans often let the number of goods they accumulate function as the measurement of their success and importance. This phenomenon is easily observable in Black youth in my classroom over the years. I have asked young Black students, "Who is worthy of respect?" Invariably, most students recognized that their parents or guardians are worthy of respect because, at the very least, they provide their basic needs. But beyond their immediate households, the people they felt were most worthy of respect were invariably people who were rich and famous. When I asked them the logic behind selecting famous entertainers as worthy of respect, they said they made a lot of money and were thus successful. Beyond entertainers, they listed people like Bill Gates. Gates did not make their list because he is the founder of a company whose software dominates almost every computer in the world; they listed him because he is worth billions of dollars. By their logic, if Bill Gate's products were still as widely used as they are today, but let us say only earned him as much as a public school teacher's salary, he would not be worthy of respect.

With this logic in mind, it is not difficult to see why so many youths look up to various questionably moral people. You might call a drug dealer or rapper who promotes (intentionally or not) violence and misogyny as evil, but to the kids that admire them, they are getting paid, so that makes them successful.

Perhaps America's education system's greatest tragedy is that it does not fill Black students' minds with an accurate depiction of themselves based on their history of accomplishments, creativity, compassion, and power. This absence of information creates a void in Black students often filled by the images projected by White-controlled corporate America, who has no vested interest in seeing

Black youth become a powerful force that can threaten their reign in the future.

While the development of a consciousness of Black history is not a panacea for all that ails Black youth, it can certainly be an effective weapon in the battle to reclaim young Black minds from feelings of powerlessness, low self-esteem, and lack of purpose. Because Black students have had so little exposure to their own history, which is replete with Black people accomplishing the seemingly impossible, they are limited in their conception of what they, as well as Black people as a whole, are capable of. If educators exposed Black students to Black people's success throughout the Diaspora, they would stand a significantly better chance of becoming conscious and believing that they have the power to control their personal lives and influence the larger society.

Lesson 7: Sumo Wrestlers & Supermodels

W e have covered what an education is and why teachers and students need a basic understanding of Black history as a fundamental component of that education. Now we turn to how to teach Black children.

To create the educational experience that Black students need, we need to adopt a pedagogical philosophy and practices tailored specifically for Black students. The African-centered or Afrocentric educational philosophy is such a model. The African-centered model requires that Black students look at the world with Africa and her Black descendants as its center. However, it is important for the reader to understand that the African-centered educational philosophy is not merely the same thing as a Eurocentric one but with Black people taking the place of White people in an irrationally superior position. The goals of an African-centered education are as follows:

1. To change the self-image of African people, eliminating any sense of inferiority based on race, class or gender, and developing a view of ourselves as whole, capable human beings.

2. To restore a way of thinking, speaking and acting which upholds the sacredness of nature and the harmony, balance and order of its parts (the principles of Ma'at) (Marks & Tonso, 2006, pp. 491492).

47

African-centered education requires a shift in practice as well as content and does not have the exclusion of any peoples as a tenet.

The curriculum and instruction in African-centered education are intended to make students rethink and reorient their ideology, values, and behavior. "African-entered curriculum stresses that educators encourage African American children to look at the world through an African-centered set of lenses that provides them with vision that is more focused, has a wider periphery, and more depth" (Lomotey, 1993, p. 456).

In addition to changing what Black children learn, African-centered education requires teachers to rethink how they view and interact with their Black students. It requires educators to create a school climate that is warm and supportive and one that demands that educators see Black children as willing and able learners historically connected to a long line of scholars and their work (Lomotey, 1993).

African-centered education also requires that educators find ways to make learning relevant to Black children's lives as Black children often see their educational experiences as separate from their real lives. African-centered education "...requires all educators to realize that academic achievement in and of itself is not enough. They must identify culturally with African American children to teach them about their culture, about life, and about where they fit in society and the world (Lomotey, 1993, p. 457).

For a teacher to be effective in an African-centered educational setting, they must recognize that Black children are different in many ways from their counterparts from other races. There are real cultural differences that prohibit a one-size-fits-all approach to education from creating a positive learning environment for all students regardless of their race. Potential teachers' lack of education about Black students' culture is a major deficiency in teacher education programs. Teachers cannot consistently and successfully educate Black students unless they understand how they view the world. Often teachers who struggle to effectively teach Black students are quick to write off their failures as the result of deficiencies in their Black students' culture. Too often, Black students are victims of the practices of educational professionals who use a "deficit-oriented" perspective to explain why they cannot get their Black students to achieve as highly as their White students (Spencer, Noll, Stoltzfus, and Harpalani, 2001, p. 21). When White students fail to meet their teacher's behavioral and educational expectations, their teachers do not blame deficient White culture for the students' failures (Ladson-Billings, 2006). In many cases, White teachers are not even aware that they come from a different culture from that of their students. Gloria Ladson-Billings, reflecting on her experiences in training teachers, noted that:

> Culture is regularly used as a code word for difference and perhaps deviance in the world of teacher education...most of my students are white, middle-class, monolingual Midwesterners. They are surrounded by people who look, talk, and perhaps think as they do. When I try to get them to think about their culture, they are stymied. They describe themselves as having "no culture" or being "just regular" or "just normal" (Ladson-Billings, 2006, p. 4).

Some people refuse to recognize differences in culture because they assume that to do so implies inequality. But there are real differences in children's cultures that teachers must make themselves aware of to succeed. It is foolish to think that a Black child growing up in the central ward of Newark, New Jersey has the same worldview and educational needs as a White child in rural Moline, Kansas. Of course, there is some common educational ground for students regardless of where they come (e.g., books, instructors, classrooms, et cetera.). However, the differences lie in how schools can use those tools most effectively to create a first-rate educational experience for students.

To use an analogy, both a supermodel and a sumo wrestler have common needs of food, exercise, and clothing to do their jobs well. However, if the sumo wrestler follows the supermodel's diet and lifestyle, he will be a phenomenal failure and likewise for a supermodel that adheres to a sumo wrestler's lifestyle. Neither the supermodel nor sumo wrestler's way of life is superior to the other. However, neither can be successful without following a course of action that is designed specifically for their individual needs. The greatest sumo wrestler trainer will ultimately be a failure if he is asked to train supermodels for the demands of that life. This is not because he is lacking in skill, but because sumo wrestlers and supermodels have almost polar opposite goals for their bodies. In Lesson 1 we stated that the purpose of education is power. But Black students and White students have different goals for that power. For most White students, the status quo in education can function fairly well because their goal is to fit into and maintain the current power structure of America. For Black students, the goal of their education needs to be the obtainment of power. There is no way that you can effectively teach these two groups of students in the same manner. In short, you cannot give the same directions to two people trying to get to different end points.

In the 1960s, the Student Non-Violent Coordinating Committee (SNCC) opened what they dubbed "Freedom Schools" in the South. At these schools, SNCC workers taught the Black community how to view the world from their own perspective instead of their oppressors'. They also taught them how the political system worked and how they can manipulate it to address their communities' needs. The effect was that Black youth packed the freedom schools because they were appreciative of the opportunity to receive an education at all and were even more pleased to receive an education that was relevant to their immediate existence (Carmichael & Thelwell, 2003).

As a result of creating a school that was in tune with the Black community's needs, SNCC had an abundance of young, eager Black minds waiting to be educated by them. Kwame Toure (formerly known as Stokely Carmichael) recollected in his autobiography that he knew that the Black students they were targeting would be excited about the school they created:

> See, I'd knew that the students would be turned-on. How not? Learning all the things that about their world, their country, and their history that the state's Bantu educational

system deliberately kept from them? And especially in an uncensored, student-centered, creative classroom situation. So we'd made the curriculum political and cultural. A lot of Black and African history and culture. A lot of discussion of Mississippi politics, the challenge, etc. Exposure to a lot of poetry, plays, and music with strong encouragement to create and perform their own. So I knew the students would have to like it (Carmichael & Thelwell, 2003, p. 387).

Carmichael recalled that teachers were awakened at 6 a.m. by knocks on their door at one school. Their initial reaction was fear as they thought it was the Ku Klux Klan coming for them. Instead, it was just eager Black students ready to learn (Carmichael & Thelwell, 2003).

An African-centered education allows educators to give the proper directions to their Black students on their journey toward freedom. Though it requires that teachers, administrators, and students rethink all of their past practices, it will lead to the ultimate goal of the development of Black students into a cadre of thinkers, workers, scholars, and organizers capable of changing African people's social, economic, and political status (Marks & Tonso, 2006, pp. 491-492). It is a remedy for schools' one-size-fits all approach to education that has been obliterating Black children by sending them into a world of Sumo wrestlers built and thinking like supermodels.

Lesson 8: You Can't Teach People You Fear

ear and education cannot exist in the same place at the same time. Sadly I have witnessed many teachers who were simply afraid of the Black students they were charged to teach. I previously stated that Black children and White children have differences based on their socio-historical backgrounds. However, one of the many things that they still both have in common is that they are children who view the world and the people in it as children do. Therefore, Black children need adults' affirmation and encouragement, just like any other children.

I can often tell how good a new teacher will be in the classroom from a straightforward test: Can they have a half-hour conversation with their students about anything other than school? That may seem like a simple task, but it reveals quite a bit about the teacher. If a teacher can have that 30-minute conversation with a group of students, they know enough about the students' world and interests to keep a conversation going. That means when they are teaching their subject matter, they will likely be able to connect their lessons to things to which the students can relate. More importantly, having that conversation means that teacher is comfortable spending time with the students as human beings instead of widgets to be worked on as part of a job.

Too often, though, teachers impose their negative biases and misconceptions about Black people on the children they teach. Those biases lead to teachers believing that their Black students are less moral and more dangerous than other students. A study from Yale University revealed that teachers are more likely to expect bad behavior from Black students. In the study, researchers showed teachers a video of a multiracial classroom setting where none of the students were actually misbehaving. When the researchers asked the teachers to identify the student that demonstrated potentially challenging behavior, 42% of the teachers identified the black boy in the video as showing behavior that could be troublesome (Young, 2016). That means that teachers look for bad behavior from Black boys, and when there is none, they invent it. When teachers bring negative preconceived notions of Black children to the classroom, they burden Black students with the unfair task of learning while also proving their humanity and morality to their teachers.

...teachers look for bad behavior from Black boys, and when there is none, they invent it.

It is important to remember that America's institutions reflect the larger society and all of its prejudices. America has a long history of presenting Black people as subhumans with questionable morals. It takes no effort to find television, movie, and music programming that perpetuates Black people's image as hyper-violent brutes. Seventy-nine percent of American teachers are White, while Black teachers only make up 8% of the nation's teaching force (National Council on Educational Statistics, 2020). Given America's still mostly segregated housing patterns, it is likely that many of these teachers have had little meaningful contact with Black people during their lives. As a result, their first impressions of Black children are not based on real-life experiences with them, but rather from a hodgepodge of information and images from pop culture. It is no surprise, then, that some teachers subconsciously bring negative perceptions of Black children to the classroom.

It is important to note, as well, that often even Black teachers that come from middle and upper-middle-class backgrounds possess the same subconscious negative biases toward their Black students that their White counterparts have. The Black experience in America is diverse, and the culture and experiences of a middle-class Black teacher can vary wildly from that of a more impoverished Black student (Kunjufu, 2002). To their demise, Black teachers who erroneously assume that every kid in their classroom should behave and view the world in the same way they do often join in with the chorus of teachers who complain about Black students' moral shortcomings.

To successfully teach Black children, a teacher must grant them the same patience, assumptions of goodness, and belief in their intellect that they would give to their own children or the children in their own neighborhood. I have had too many discussions with teachers that use the phrase "these kids" to delineate the Black children they teach from the "normal" children in their lives. It was not uncommon throughout my career to hear comments like, "These kids don't want to do any work" or "These kids don't know how to act."

I remember a teacher complaining that 80% of his kids failed a test, which led him to say, "These kids don't care about school." Any halfway decent teacher in this scenario would instantly know that if 80% of their students failed a test, the teacher is the problem, not the students. If a McDonald's restaurant had 80% of its customers complain about its food one day, the manager would not come to the conclusion that "these costumers" just do not know how to eat the right way. They would rightfully conclude that they had serviced their clientele incorrectly and need to change.

Teachers cannot go into any classroom, thinking that their students are naturally deficient in any way. Black children are often desperate for relationships with adults who believe that they are worthy of love and believe in their abilities. A teacher can change a child's entire life by uttering a few encouraging words at the right moment. A teacher who fears their students has no chance of ever inspiring their students as their fear is a constant insult to the children in their classroom that dehumanizes them into negative stereotypes.

Sadly, it is common for institutions to perceive Black children as older and more sinister than they are. The criminal justice system, for instance, charges Black children with adult level crimes more than they do White children. In New Jersey, where I live, about 87% of the youth tried as adults are African American or Latino even though national research shows White kids commit the same amount of crimes that prosecutors could waive up to the adult system. Prosecutors, however, simply do not attempt to try white kids as adults at the same rates (WNYC News, 2016).

American society also erodes Black girls' childhoods much earlier in life than they do White girls. A Georgetown University study showed that people assume that Black girls need to be nurtured, protected, and comforted less than White girls. The study showed that people also assume that Black girls know more about adult topics and sex than White girls. Schools' denial of Black girls' innocence leads to harsher punishments when disciplinary issues arise (Epstein, R., Blake, J., & Gonzalez, T. 2019).

Teachers should be the antidote to the sickness that distorts people's perception of Black children. The teacher's function should always be to protect their Black students' childhoods, not rob them of it.

Lesson 9: Teaching is Art, Not Science

One of the most consistently frustrating experiences I have had as a teacher is listening to administrators reduce good teaching to a checklist of mostly clerical actions. Too many educational leaders have the same fantasy where they create great teachers by making them write unnecessarily long lesson plans, create fancy bulletin boards, move lockstep with the curriculum, and complete all the extra paperwork required by whatever data-based fad has just been sold to them by a consultant.

There is no one recipe for creating a great teacher. Teaching is not a science; it is an art. In science, one can readily reproduce results. If you drop water's temperature to below freezing, it will turn to ice every single time; this is not true of teachers. Two teachers can have the same training, lesson plans, and students, and one can be a spectacular failure while the other is a huge success.

It is much more useful to look at the development of good teachers as the same process of developing good artists. There may be basic common skills that every student has to master in an art school, but you would not expect every artist to paint the same picture in the same way. Two painters may start with the same type of canvas and use the same type of paint to create their work, but beyond that, they have the freedom to get to the goal of completing the work in their unique way. In the end, they might end up with two pieces of work that are absolutely nothing alike but are both masterpieces.

The teacher-as-an-artist analogy also works because it describes the work conditions of teachers. One of the things that makes an artist is the decisions they make to reach their goals within the constraints of their available resources. Graffiti artists learn how to create masterpieces given their constraints of only having access to concrete and brick walls and spray paint. They use their constraints as a springboard to creativity.

Photographers, too, are continually making choices within the constraints of physics. A photographer can shoot at high speeds that will keep every subject sharp in their photos but at the expense of making the entire image darker. They can balance out the lack of light by raising a camera's ISO level. However, that can create grain and other artifacts that will make the final image appear less clear. Photography is all about making decisions on which of these settings the photographer is going to adjust, knowing the offsetting negative effect.

Every photographer has their preference for balancing this exposure triangle, but there is never a singular correct way to do it. It all depends on what the photographer is shooting, the particular look they are aiming for, the photographer's skill set, and the camera's limitations. The intentional choices photographers make given the constraints we just described are what makes them artists.

Teachers are the same. They operate within constraints of time, resources, personal skill, and students' abilities and interests. None of those factors are static from teacher to teacher. Just as there is no one-size-fits-all curriculum for students, there is no one-size-fits-all way to teach. Every teacher has to be the best artist they can be by making the best choices possible, given the constraints they are working under, to create their works of art on their student canvases.

Lesson 10: The Smartest Guy in the Room

Every kid in a classroom needs a win. Teachers always reaffirm students that raise their hands and answer questions correctly and get good grades on tests. However, every single kid in a classroom needs at least one moment where they get to be the proverbial "smartest guy in the room." They require a moment when they get to show off their expertise in something–anything.

Every kid needs that occasional morale boost of being the best at something. Many of my past students needed the shot of confidence that comes from an adult celebrating any particle of excellence they have in them. A wise teacher once told me, "Students will forget much of the details of what you taught them when they grow old, but they will never forget how you made them feel."

So as a teacher, you have to go out of your way to make each kid in your class feel good about something that they are or do. That may mean creating an assignment that requires the students to draw a picture so that the quiet artistic kid in the back of the class gets a chance to be the room's star. It may mean asking that kid that is always rambling on about pop culture news to explain to you what the hottest new artist is and why you should care. It may mean going to watch one of your students in a school play or athletic event and

The simple act of truly seeing each student–even for the briefest of moments–will mean the world to that student.

then talking about how proud you are of them in front of the entire class the next day.

The simple act of truly seeing each student—even for the briefest of moments—will mean the world to that student. They will remember that there is at least one place in the giant concrete building that the state legally compels them to enter each day where they are noticed and celebrated for their gifts. They will remember that you cared enough to at least attempt to connect with them. They will remember how you made them feel.

I have had countless students tell me that they work harder in the classes where they have teachers they "like." Bad teachers dismiss this critical information by saying, "I am not here to be the students' friend. I am here to give them information that I already know, and they don't." But that represents a fundamental misunderstanding of what students mean when they say they "like a teacher." What that student is really saying is, "I like the way that teacher makes me feel about myself."

A teacher that consciously makes students feel good about who they are does not have to lower their academic or classroom decorum standards. It merely requires that they make a deliberate effort to find ways to celebrate some level of success in each student. This practice's effect is students with more confidence that put more effort into their work because of their rapport with their teacher. You can rarely intimidate a student into greatness, but you can often push them to the next level by validating their sense of worth.

Lesson 11: The Myth of Classroom Control

The hardest part of teaching has nothing to do with any academic content. The challenge of teaching is getting 20-30 young people (who often have no desire to be in school) to listen and respond to everything you say for 180 days or so each year. It does not matter how knowledgeable you are on your subject matter or how many degrees you have to your name. You could be the world's most foremost authority in your discipline, but that is no guarantee that a single teenager will have any interest in listening to a single word that you have to say.

Every teacher deals with the challenge of getting dozens of often disinterested young people to follow them every day of the school year. This task of getting a classroom full of students to do what you want them to do when you want them to do it is often called classroom management or control. Classroom management is, by far, the most difficult part of teaching. One of the factors that exiting teachers site in their decision to leave the profession is student discipline issues (Edsal, 2019). Teachers in schools that are primarily populated by students of color quit their jobs at a rate 70% higher than teachers at schools with predominately White student bodies.

Many teachers make the mistake of entering a classroom under the assumption that their teacher's title will automatically garner respect and compliance from their students. Huge mistake. In the 21st Century, many Black children have witnessed numerous adults not worthy of trust or respect. The authority figures they see in political, justice, and educational systems often behave in ways that are detrimental to their well-being. When a teacher walks into a room, there is no guarantee that the students will view them as any worthier of their respect than any other random person.

My moment of clarity on classroom management was delivered to me by one of my teaching mentors. She sat me down one day and explained that classroom control or management is just a myth, a magic trick. The teacher is never in control of the classroom. The students outnumber the teacher 20 or even 30 to 1 on any given day. If thirty students all decide to do something, there is nothing that a single teacher in a classroom can do about it. The numbers just do not add up.

Since the students have all the power due to their sheer numbers, the teacher has to convince them to surrender their classroom power and control. Excellent teachers solve this problem of power imbalance by offering this trade: *In exchange for your power and control, I will give you information that is so engaging, so empowering, it is in your best interest to surrender control of the room.* In short, the teacher has to convince the students that the payoff for letting go of their power is greater than the payoff for holding on to it.

Convincing students that you have something worthwhile to teach them is more difficult than one would think. I remember looking out of my classroom door during one of my prep periods and seeing two students dancing in the hallway to distorted music blaring from their cell phones. They were registered for a class during the period but felt it unnecessary to go, so here they were, in front of my door, choosing to show off their educated feet instead of their educated minds.

Every halfway decent teacher knows that the most critical word in classroom management is "why." Why is that student behaving in that manner? Why are those students dancing in the hallway instead of reading in class? Perhaps the problem is that they feel more reward in dancing in the hallway outside of class than in actually being in the classroom. What pains me the most (given the teacher that I knew they had that period) is that they may actually have

Every halfway decent teacher knows that the most critical word in classroom management is "why."

been right. There is a chance that nothing remotely relevant to their lives was happening in their scheduled class. Of course, our hallway-dancing students should have followed their assigned schedule. However, we also have to recognize that their teacher failed to sell these two young people on the value of their class, and I believe that is an experience shared by Black students all across America.

For schools to have classes that engage Black students, they must hire and train teachers who understand their students' culture. Teachers need to understand that culture is more than just an individual's customs, language, artifacts, and physical environment. One's history, social experience, values, and beliefs are equally important in forming the core of a culture. Therefore, understanding one's culture is to understand their worldview or ideology (Anderson, 1992). Chapters 2 and 3 in this book are long expositions on history because, without that historical context, it is impossible for teachers to accurately understand how their Black students view the world.

Without understanding Black students' worldview, teachers cannot figure out ways to connect their lessons to them.

When teachers truly understand how their Black students view the world and what is important to them, they can easily tailor their teaching and curriculum in a way that will make them gladly make the trade of student power for teacher knowledge.

Year in and year out, I have been able to convince my students to acquiesce their power to me because I promise that if they follow my program, I guarantee that I will change the way they look at the world forever. One of Black students' consistent desires is for teachers to finally teach them the full truth of their own history. By the time they reach my high school history class, they are wise enough to know that most of the history their schools have exposed them to erroneously portrays them as secondary characters in America's story. I make them the promise that I will expose them to the real story of America in exchange for their collective classroom power. The key is that I have the knowledge and skill to make good on that promise. If a teacher cannot deliver the goods, the deal is off, and their students will take the classroom back.

Every teacher needs to deeply examine why a student should listen to anything they have to say. A teacher has to offer more to a student than a lame explanation that "this information may be useful one day." Black students work better when they know that there is a clear payoff for their expected labor (Kunjufu, 2002).

Nevertheless, no matter how engaging a teacher's content may be, from time to time, teachers are going to have to redirect the behavior of their students–there is no getting around that. This is when the other factor in getting students to follow a teacher's lead comes into play–the student-teacher relationship. An author once said, "Rules without relationship leads to rebellion" (McDowell, 2020). This adage could not possibly be more true in the classroom. A teacher who criticizes or even corrects a student who is a stranger to them will receive a defensive response. Students need to know that you care about them before they will listen to any critiques you have of them. There is a difference between someone's best friend telling them that their outfit looks horrible and they need to go home and change versus a complete stranger delivering the same message. A person hearing that message from a friend will understand that it comes from a place of love and concern. A person might receive that message from a stranger as only an insult because they have no context to judge the stranger's intention.

> *Students need to know that you care about them before they will listen to any critiques you have of them.*

The teacher's relationship with their students is the greatest weapon in their arsenal. When a teacher with genuine relationships with their students offers praise or criticism, it falls on receptive ears because they know that their teacher would not intentionally insult or misguide them. Teachers who have this relationship firmly established do not have to waste energy yelling or arguing with off-task classes. When my classes are not meeting my standard, I simply have to express my sincere disappointment in my students' actions, and it usually hits them like a sledgehammer. When someone who has consistently supported and advocated for them now withdraws that affection and expresses disappointment, it makes them immediately take stock of their actions.

Yelling at students, writing misbehaving kids' names on the board, threatening to call mischievous students' parents, or sending disruptive students to the principal's office are ineffectual techniques in the longterm. America has exposed Black students to enough scary things in their lives that a teacher yelling at them or the specter of suspension from school is completely unintimidating and unmotivating. However, they will run through a wall to maintain respect from a teacher that genuinely cares about them.

Ultimately, a teacher should not desire to *control* a classroom of young humans as if they were a heard of cattle. It is the job of teachers to *lead* a classroom of young minds to reach their full potential. There is no shortcut to mastering the magic trick of classroom management. Teachers have to do the daily work of building meaningful relationships with their students before building up their minds.

Lesson 12: Check Your Armor at the Door

Even though they are masters of disguise, many Black students are simmering with anger–and justifiably so. Being Black in America demands the development of coping mechanisms to deal with the extra stress that comes from daily encounters with overt and subvert White supremacy. When one combines the demands of living with White supremacy with the challenges of poverty, life becomes even more stressful. Black children across America's classrooms may do a masterful job of masking their stress, but rest assured it is there, affecting them every day.

Centuries of intentional White supremacist governmental policies have helped to create Black communities with children living in poverty at rates four times that of White children (Bowman, Comer & Johns, 2018). Nevertheless, the students that I have taught year after year have continued to walk into my classroom each day with smiles on their faces. But when class is over, many of those same students stay behind and talk to me about what is happening in their lives and their masks come off.

I have had students share stories about their parents, who abandoned them to look for drugs. I have had multiple students that have been victims of rape and sexual assault. I have had students that are working almost full-time hours to support their families. I have had students that have been forced to live with physically and psychologically abusive relatives. I have had students that lost their homes in the middle of a school year and were forced to live in homeless shelters. And I have taught thousands of students who depend on their school to provide the majority of their meals.

Sometimes these students will come into a classroom with a less than jolly disposition. Teachers have to understand that no matter how much their students may smile on a regular basis, they will have days where they just cannot pretend any longer that the burdens they are carrying do not hurt. A student may come to class and put their head down on a desk. In this situation, teachers have to have the ability to discern between a student that is taking the day off out of laziness and the one that is trying their best to keep their whole being from breaking down in front of the class.

Teachers have to understand that no matter how much their students may smile on a regular basis, they will have days where they just cannot pretend any longer that the burdens they are carrying do not hurt.

I have watched so many novice teachers wreck a classroom's culture by assuming the worse when they see a student acting in a way that the teacher deems unacceptable. Teachers have to develop that sixth sense that tells you to leave that student with their head down alone. A teacher demanding that the student pick their head up and pay attention to them is making the wrong move. Embarrassing a student who is already having a bad day because they are dealing with problems that no child should carry will blow up in that teacher's face in spectacular fashion.

The smarter and more compassionate way to handle the situation is to find a moment to talk to that student in private to find out what is happening in their life outside of the classroom. I have found that students are extremely appreciative of teachers who show compassion when they see them disengaged and in pain instead of assuming the student is insolent.

Since I was well aware of the challenges that many of my students faced outside of school, on the first day of the school year, I preemptively address any issues they may have that might affect the way they carry themselves in my classroom. I explain that I know that many of them have had more stress in their lives as teenagers than most adults will have in their entire lives. I tell them that I know that for some of them, just the fact that they get up every morning and still feel motivated enough to come to school is a victory. I am aware that some of my students come from circumstances where they have to wear armor made of aggressiveness and defensiveness to survive. My classroom, however, is a safe zone where none of the protective psychological mechanisms that students often carry with them are needed. They can check their suit of armor at the door, and for at least one period a day, they can be as happy and as nerdy as they want without consequence. After class, they can put their armor back on to face the world. A classroom should be a child's oasis rather than an additional battlefield.

Lesson 13: Every Child Is an Artist

One of the obvious places Black people have thrived in America is in the arts. Albert Einstein stated, "I am enough of an artist to draw freely upon my imagination. Imagination is more important than knowledge. Knowledge is limited. Imagination encircles the world" (Nilsson, 2020). Despite the power and importance of the arts, many adults encourage Black children to see them as just hobbies instead of a proper career path. People's disparaging of art careers is tragic as the arts have often provided Black people's loudest and most influential voices.

The people that love them are often aspiring artists' biggest hindrance. Pablo Picasso said, "Every child is an artist. The problem is how to remain an artist once we grow up." Parents and friends of young artists often try to convince them that, at worst, they have no future in the arts, and at best, if a future in art does exist, it is not a meaningful one. These same art-discouragers will spend hours talking about their favorite movies, television programs, and music. They love the arts, but they inadvertently insult young artists they love by implying that while the arts are great, we do not believe that *you* can be great enough at it to earn a living.

Despite the popular myth of the starving artist, the unemployment rate for art graduates is half that of the national average

Despite the popular myth of the starving artist, the unemployment rate for art graduates is half that of the national average, and 71% of bachelor's degree holders in the arts and 86% of those with master's degrees are working or have worked as professional artists (Americans for the Arts, 2020). Meanwhile, a law school graduate in 2011, for instance, was only 55% likely to be employed in a law-related field (Henderson, 2012). Life and the economy are unpredictable, but being an artist does not make you less advantaged than people with degrees in other fields.

Part of the problem here is that people tend to separate art from the so-called "real" part of school. I have had many conversations with non-artists that view the arts as a non-intellectual endeavor during my career. They view artistic ability as a natural talent instead of a skill developed by countless hours of work and study over many years.

I counter that the highest form of intelligence is creation. There is nothing more intellectually exhausting (or rewarding) than engaging in the process of taking something from non-existence to existence. As Neil Gaiman said, "The world always seems brighter when you've just made something that wasn't there before." It is not an accident that the highest education levels require students to create new and original knowledge. Students earning Ph.D.'s, for instance, have to essentially create an original book of knowledge in order to graduate. Artists engage in the creation of original work all of the time. They have an amazing ability to envision something in their minds and then bring that thought into existence in the physical world. Imagining something that does not actually exist and then bringing it to life requires supreme intelligence.

Cognitive science researcher, George Lakoff, argues that the brain responds to images of objects and actions in much the same way as real-life experiences (Lakoff, 2014). So a picture of a beautiful sunset makes your brain react in a similar way as watching a real sunset. This is important as it means that artists' can use their work as a powerful tool to make people feel things that they cannot personally experience. In the 1960s, Dr. King took advantage of the art form of film to capture the pain of Black protestors that were bitten by dogs and knocked down with fire hoses to gain empathy from millions of people around the world who were not there to experience the event. A more common example is the work of professional sports photographers. They capture moments in events that make the viewer feel like they are participants in the action they are viewing. In short, art can serve as a virtual reality simulator for experiences.

Art has always been critical to Black people's survival in America. For most of Black people's existence in America, mainstream White America systematically shut them out of upward mobility avenues except for sports and entertainment. Consequently, often the most famous representatives of the thoughts of the Black community have been athletes and entertainers. Howard Bryant points out that White people were unwilling to listen to people like the first Black Rhodes Scholar, Alain Locke, despite having studied at Oxford, The University of Berlin, and earning a Ph.D. from Harvard. White American culture offered no platform for a man of Locke's abilities. However, it did leave the door slightly open for athletes and entertainers to be seen and heard, and they capitalized on the opportunity (Bryant, 2018). Legendary athlete and entertainer, Paul Robeson, born in 1898, never ceased to use his platform as an athlete, singer, and actor to offer direct and overt criticism of the blatant racism that Americans embedded into their daily lives.

Robeson's mantle was taken up by scores of Black artists in every decade since who recognized the nature of art requires artists to always envision the creation of things that don't exist yet. It is no surprise that music and visual art have accompanied every revolution. Famed actor Ossie Davis once said, "Any form of art is a form of power; it has impact, it can affect change - it can not only move us, it makes us move."

Discouraging Black students from pursuing the arts is detrimental to the larger society and personally harmful to the individual. Oscar Wilde said, "One can exist without art, but one cannot live without it." When someone is an artist, art is at the core of their identity. They view and interact with the world through the lens of art. Art is not something they do; it is something they are. Taking away art from an artist means stripping the soul out of a young person and denying them the chance to be their true self. They will exist, but they will never live in the fullness of who they really are or could be.

Lesson 14: Don't Use Black Kids As Your Step Stool

This lesson is extremely simple: Teachers should not take a job teaching in a Black community simply because they could not find a job in the suburban district where they really wanted to work. Teachers that do this are immoral. They are not heroes who decided to spend some time serving underprivileged youth. They are selfishly exploiting America's teacher shortage for a temporary buck.

I have always said that teaching is not a job; it is a way of life. To be an effective teacher, you have to give every fiber of your being to your students for nearly 200 days of the year. You simply cannot do that while you have one foot out the door. Beyond that, teaching is not like working in a factory where you are constructing some inanimate object.

It is cruel not to bother to learn who your students are as amazingly unique people rather than some objects you throw information at each day because you have no intention of staying long. Many things are replaceable in life, but time is not one of them. Teachers that deliver a poor performance in the classroom are potentially wasting almost an entire year of their students' lives. Additionally, a callous teacher can scar young people in ways that never completely heal.

The students that teachers work with are humans that form feelings and attachments to them. I like to remind parents that I spend more time with their children in most cases than they do. As such, it is my responsibility to build meaningful positive relationships with each of my students.

When you build those relationships with students, it is cruel to throw them away out of personal convenience. Every person should be free to work and live wherever they can, but its cold-hearted to lead students on by making them believe that you have a longterm interest in them when you know that you are actively trying to get away from them as quickly as possible.

Black children deserve to be more than some broke teacher's consolation prize. They are not practice-children for teachers to use while they gain their official licensure, earn a salary and benefits, and get experience to add to their resume to make themselves more appealing for their next job. Black children deserve to have teachers in their classrooms who are fully committed to them and not people who run away at the first sign that students are not receiving them as a Hollywood-style-White-Messiah -teacher-movie hero.

Lesson 15: Controlling Black Bodies

One of my continuing frustrations during my career has been schools' administration and faculty prioritizing controlling Black bodies over freeing their minds. I have sat through countless staff meetings listening to teachers complain about their students' behavior, clothes, cell phone usage, language, and hallway demeanor. But I have been to very few meetings where those same teachers devote any energy to discussing how to make the curriculum more relevant and engaging for their students.

I fully understand that schools cannot function effectively without a certain level of order. However, I also understand that student behavior is inseparable from the quality and relevance of the instruction they receive. As we discussed in a previous chapter, students take their power back when they feel they are not getting anything worthwhile from the teacher. Therefore, teachers and administrators should primarily focus on engaging their students' minds, but that has been an afterthought for many of them in my experience.

Urban schools seem to have an unspoken understanding that they have to subdue the student population to educate it. I sat in meetings the morning after the public revelation of egregious acts of racist police brutality and grand jury refusals to indict the offending police officers where teachers never attempt to discuss what that means for the Black children in their classrooms. Yet they ramble on endlessly about how to get students to sit up straighter or talk less in their classes.

Too much focus is on the physical in Black schools. In New Jersey, where I teach, only failing urban public school districts require their students to wear uniforms. The rationale given by school leaders is that uniforms prevent students from focusing on fashion instead of learning, and kids will not feel the social pressure that comes with having to own the most fashionable clothing. They also claim that uniforms stop students from wearing gang-affiliated clothing and from displaying inappropriate messages on their bodies. All of this is supposed to lead to students being better and more focused scholars.

My problem with this line of thinking is that if uniforms are this amazing panacea for education problems, why are only predominately low-income Black and Latino school districts utilizing them? The wealthiest school districts in the state do not want more focused students? Why are they not adopting this same amazing revolutionary policy?

Maybe it is because school leaders are making the subtle argument that there is something different about Black and Latino children that is a little less civilized than their White counterparts. There seems to be an assumption that Black children cannot empathize with classmates who have less money than they do and thus less fashionable clothing. Apparently, black kids need external help in the form of slightly more formal clothing to help them concentrate in class, whereas White kids do not have that problem. White children's parents presumably have the ability to make sure that their children come to school with no inappropriate clothing on. However, Black schools' uniform policies imply that Black parents do not have that same skill. At its best, public school uniforms represent a band-aid on issues that schools inadequately address. At its worst, they are the physical representation of urban schools' habit of compensating for their lack of success elevating children's minds by over-regulating their bodies.

Black students have repeatedly shared with me that they feel like their schools resemble a prison more than a school. Sometimes out of reasonable caution, and other times out of borderline paranoia, security can override the mission of educating young people in Black urban schools. One wonders how much focus

Black students have repeatedly shared with me that they feel like their schools resemble a prison more than a school.

students lose when they have to walk through metal detectors each day or get wanded by security officers and police.

Again, sometimes these measures are necessary, but sometimes they feel like overkill. For instance, I remember one year, a pair of my school's security officers performed their ordered duty of executing a random body and bag check in one of my classes. It just so happened that the period they came into my classroom was my AP history class. The security officers approached a girl a few months away from graduating as the school's valedictorian. I watched in amazement as she stood up, got patted down, and had her bag checked without even stopping the conversation she was having with the girl next to her. A daily existence where even the most innocuous kids in the building still have to get treated as potential threats was unsettling to me. What was most disturbing was how my students thought this was normal for a school.

Sadly, my experiences are not unique in America. There are numerous scholars and educators concerned with the criminalization of Black student bodies. An administrator in a Boston school reflected on the potential harm he was doing to his students each day as he performed security checks on them upon their entrance:

I am an administrator at a public high school in Boston, serving almost entirely low-income black and Latino students, and that means every morning I am the white guy at the metal detector telling them they are suspected of a crime as they walk into their school (Stumacher, 2020).

There are legitimate, serious threats in schools that require them to curtail some liberties at times. However, as educators, we have to do a better job striking a balance between safety and freedom. What happens in a school day that balances out the negativity bred from schools starting a kid's day as a potential threat to their own community? Suppose we have to have draconian security measures for students before they can get access to their school. In that case, we should at least provide an amazingly uplifting experience once they get in.

Instead, schools often meet Black children with more intense control of their bodies once they enter the building. Administrators and teachers bark out orders to stay to the hallway's right and give out demerits for having some part of their uniform slightly out of code. Teachers call security on them for trivial matters like talking too much in class or voicing their opposition to what or how a teacher is teaching. They get threatened with suspension for being a minute late to class. They have their lockers and bags searched by security and police officers, sometimes even by drug-sniffing dogs (Guevara, 2019). In Seattle, a teacher called the police on a Black 5th grader, whom she said verbally threatened her (Bekele, 2019).

Young people meet the expectations adults have for them. If educators want a school filled with students that comport themselves with class and dignity, they first have to create a school culture that treats them with love and respect. The security measures that schools put into place are bandaids over serious wounds. Suppose schools truly believe that their student populations are prone to acts of violence. In that case, they need to deal with their students' emotional, psychological, and social challenges that lead to violent acts. Unfortunately, even as schools increase their security budgets, they lessen their budgets for guidance and counseling departments. These cuts are tragic as properly trained guidance staff are best equipped to deal with students' root problems that result in them dealing with conflict in unproductive ways (Sitrin, 2020).

Schools ridiculously understaff their guidance departments all across America (Bidwell, 2013). Schools mistakenly view programs and staff that are not directly connected to making standardized math and English test scores higher as nonessential. In the 21st Century, the reality is that schools are no longer places just for academic learning. Urban schools will continue to fail until they become full-service centers for all of young people's needs. Schools have to be the place for students to go when they need food, physical and psychological security, knowledge, healing, exercise, peace, and love. In short, urban schools have to be ready to play every single role that a family would play. This obviously requires a radical rethinking of schools' priorities, starting with making guidance and counseling services the center of the school instead of an ancillary afterthought. Schools cannot do this necessary restructuring while they cut guidance budgets and relegate highly trained counseling professionals to mere class schedule makers.

We do not want schools that Black children attend to mirror the police's militarization that is already happening in the communities in which many of them live. At the time of this writing, there is a mass movement calling for the redistribution of the funding that goes to police forces. The goal is to have the government spend more money on mental health workers to address situations that do not require violent force. This is the same direction that urban Black schools need to go, shifting their priorities from physical security to their students' psychological and emotional security. The pain that many Black students feel from living under challenging circumstances beyond their control manifests itself in negative behaviors. Schools need to see and address that pain, not search and suspend it.

Lesson 16: You Don't Need Permission to Be Great

Teachers do not have to wait for permission to execute some of the ideas in this book. One of the pieces of advice that I give young teachers is that they should see themselves as the expert in their classroom. No one should be better-versed in teaching the particular group of students in their room 180 days out of the year. As a teacher, you cannot wait for an administrator or lead teacher to come from on high and deliver you magical pedagogical tablets. The teacher in the room has to figure it out.

If you know that you should be teaching more Black history and literature in your courses, do it. If you have some crazy, unorthodox lesson that you think might work, do it. Like we discussed before, teaching is art, and art is about making intentional choices. You have to actively make decisions to shape your classroom in the way that best suits your students.

Whether you succeed or not, do it your way. Don't ever leave yourself open to doing it someone else's way and then blame them if you fail.

Sometimes you will have to manage up. Your principal or supervisor may not always see the power of your vision until after you bring it to fruition, so you will have to put your ideas into motion yourself. Once your colleagues see the impact you have on your students, they will get on board. You first, however, have to have the courage to be the leader in your classroom.

National Football League Hall of Fame coach Tom Landry once gave this advice about coaching, which is equally true of teaching:

> Whether you succeed or not, do it your way. Don't ever leave yourself open to doing it someone else's way and then blame them if you fail (Cohen, 2014).

At the end of the day, it is your name that is on students' schedules. If they have a horrible experience with you, none of them will say, "Mr. Johnson's class was horrible, but it was not his fault because he was given an uninspired curriculum and a principal who does not like to rock the boat." They will only remember that you wasted a whole year of their lives.

Trusting yourself will mean that you will occasionally fall flat on your face. Every single good teacher has had lessons that bomb, and that is okay. Great success in the classroom also requires great risk. You will never be a good teacher if you are afraid to believe in what your instincts tell you about what the children in your classroom need. Your colleagues will generally respect you more for being a teacher who swings for the fences and misses, than one who is afraid even to go up to bat. You have to be a leader to be a teacher, and leaders have to be willing to be the first to step into the unknown.

Lesson 17: Blueprints & Black Teachers

here is no shortage of children that want to grow up to be professional athletes. Black communities have frequently lifted athletes to heroic status, much to the chagrin of some elites. Black children's desire to be athletes is perfectly logical. America seldom celebrates Black people's accomplishments outside of sports and the arts the way they do the people in them. Because athletics is one of the few places in American society that even portends to be a meritocracy, Black children get to see a plethora of examples of excellence that looks like them. Naturally, many Black children then desire to follow in the footsteps of these larger than life figures.

There is a lesson about teaching to be learned from young people's obsession with sports: students learn better when the information teachers present has real-world implications and payoffs (Kunjufu, 2002). I know that any child who tells me they will be a pro athlete is wrong for an almost certainty. For instance, the odds of a high school basketball player making it to the National Basketball Association (NBA) are minuscule. Out of the approximately 541,479 students playing high school basketball, only 46 (0.000085%) will make it to the NBA (Kerr-Dineen, 2016). These odds, however, do not stop children from chasing their hoop dreams.

Children are not discouraged by the poor odds because even though the road is ridiculously hard and improbable, the path to get to the NBA is easily viewable by potential players. They get to see real-life people in their neighborhoods practice for hours on end, work their way through the recreational leagues, AAU tournaments, high school competition, superstar summer camps and showcases, star in college programs, and then finally get drafted to the NBA. It is a road filled with attrition; nevertheless, it is a road that can be easily be seen and understood.

Because Black children can easily observe the path to success in sports, it partially explains why so many of them will invest so much effort into sports. Even though the odds are slim to none of making it to the pros, they can clearly see how each step of the process brings them closer to their desired goal. There is no mystery or magic behind success in sports. Once someone exposes Black children to the blueprint of how to reach a goal, no matter how lofty, they feel confident that they can achieve it too.

One of the problems that Black children face is that they do not have enough people in their lives from other disciplines showing them their blueprints to success. They need scientists, entrepreneurs, lawyers, and other professionals that look like them to reach back into their lives and show them the plan they followed to reach their success. Black children need these tangible Black success stories to reaffirm their abilities and show them exactly how the subjects they are studying today are directly connected to what they want to be tomorrow.

Black teachers can function as the link to other Black professionals who can come into the classroom and share their personal blueprints for success in their fields. Black students must see those successful Black professionals are not mythical creatures but are real people who come from the same circumstances as them. Black professionals demystifying how to become entrepreneurs, doctors, artists, scientists, electricians, mechanics, or information technology specialists would be an invaluable experience for Black students. Most importantly, these visits to the classroom could lead to Black students gaining mentorship opportunities, where they get expert help in executing their blueprint for their life's goals.

Good Black teachers play several critical roles in bridging the gap between where Black students are and where they want to be educationally and professionally. Eighty percent of American teachers are White (National Center for Education Statistics, 2020), so a Black teacher's mere existence in a classroom has a significant impact on Black students. Black teachers serve as conspicuous examples of Black scholarship and learning. Every single Black teacher in America's public schools is a college graduate. Black teachers in the classroom automatically provide a role model and potential mentor for Black students that can help them apply, attend, and graduate from college. The Black teacher in a Black student's classroom is concrete proof of Black academic achievement. Harvard Graduate School of Education Lecturer, Sarah Leibel stated:

> It's really important that students have people who reflect back to them their language, their culture, their ethnicity, their religion. It doesn't mean all the people in their lives have to do that mirroring, but they should have some. And we know that in the teaching profession, there really are not enough mirrors (Moss, 2016).

Studies have shown that Black students' access to Black teachers raises their reading and math test scores, graduation rates, and increases their desire to attend college. They have also reported feeling more welcomed and cared for when they are taught by teachers of color (Carver-Thomas, 2018).

When Black teachers are at their best, they shield Black children from negative biases in schools' curriculum, teachers' expectations, and culture. They fight behind the scenes to get their schools to invest in more inclusive texts, hire more Black faculty, and equitably share rewards and punishments amongst all students. Black teachers serve as a protective barrier between Black students and the unintentional and intentional slights that are ever-present in American institutions.

When Black teachers are at their best, they shield Black children from negative biases in schools' curriculum, teachers' expectations, and culture.

I love children with gigantic dreams, so I am absolutely against discouraging Black students from pursuing their athletic goals. On the contrary, I want more millionaire Black athletes that have the ear of the world. But we need to have an army of successful Black professionals in every discipline that can influence society for the better and provide the blueprints for the kids that come after them.

Lesson 18: Be a Fortune Teller

P arents always tell their children that they can be anything they want to be when they grow up if they work hard enough. This statement is only partially true. They can be anything they want to be if they work hard enough *and* have enough time. A 65-year-old man is unlikely to become an NBA rookie-of-the-year no matter how hard he works in the gym. Fortunately, for every school-aged child, they have plenty of time to reach their goals. Time is what teachers have to consider when they look at each of their students.

Teachers need to have the ability to look at a child and see not only what they are now, but also any glimmer of what they could be given enough time and effort.

Teachers need to have the ability to look at a child and see not only what they are now, but also any glimmer of what they could be given enough time and effort. One of my mentors would often tell girls in her class that showed a glimmer of potential, but were not fulfilling it academically or behaviorally, that they were diamonds in the rough. She was a great fortune teller because she could see all of her students' present flaws, but she could also see the greatness and value they possessed that was presently buried beneath unproductive beliefs and habits. Consequently, she held those students to high expectations as if they were already polished and shining for the world to see. She did not wait for them to be finished products to appreciate them; she treated those students as if they had already reached their full valuation. Like an expert stockbroker, she got in on the ground floor of their greatness before they skyrocketed to the top.

The ability to look past students' present flaws and into their potential future is extremely important when teaching Black children. Their current circumstances might be covering their diamond core with sludge and dust. However, as a teacher, you have to be able to see that glimmering speck of potential that shines when the sun hits that kid at just the right angle. You have no idea how life-changing the sowing of a single seed of belief into a student may be for a child. That one word of encouragement a teacher delivers to a student about their potential might be the singular thing that makes that student decide to fight through their current circumstances instead of quitting. Black students need teachers who never stop believing that they can always be more tomorrow than today.

Lesson 19: The Payoff

Only three types of people become teachers in Black schools: the naïve, the stupid, and the heroic. The naïve that enter into teaching simply have no idea how demanding a career in education is. The stupid that enter teaching walk in thinking that it is an easy 8 AM-3 AM job that will give them lots of free time and the summer off. The heroic that enter teaching have clear eyes and can see exactly how much of an uncelebrated struggle the rest of their adult life will be in the service of others—but do it anyhow.

Teaching is an almost entirely thankless job...When you do it well, few people notice. When you do it poorly, it feels like the world criticizes you.

Teaching is an almost entirely thankless job. As much as I love it, I would not wish it upon anyone. When you do it well, few people notice. When you do it poorly, it feels like the world criticizes you. There is almost no external motivation to become a good teacher. There is no material reward for being the best teacher in a school. You will be paid and often accorded the same amount (or lack) of respect as the worst teacher in the school. When the public criticizes your school, no one will say, "That school sucks but, oh, not you! You are great!" People consistently bash public schools with blanket statements that equate the worst people in the profession with the very same people that would do absolutely anything to get their children to learn. They lump the bad teacher together with the teacher who puts in twelve to thirteen-hour workdays planning lessons, calling parents, visiting homes, calling college admissions offices, counseling, and writing letters of recommendation. There are far more stories about bad teachers than teachers who go the extra mile for their students.

Teachers frequently come across people that make assumptions about what they do that are completely unfounded. There is a perception that somehow teaching is easy. One idiot, famously said, "Those that can, do; those that can't, teach." Everyone then has a great laugh at teachers' expense.

The reality is that teaching is more difficult than doing. Teaching requires one to already possess the skills and knowledge that they are trying to impart. They must also understand their ability and skill so thoroughly that they can systematically break it into parts that the completely uninitiated can understand and then do themselves.

A practical example of the difficulty of teaching is the failure of legendary NBA superstar Magic Johnson's foray into coaching. Johnson was so frustrated with his inability to get his players on the same page as himself that at one practice, he took a player's electronic pager that started beeping in the middle of a conversation and smashed it to pieces (Dwyer, 2015). He only lasted sixteen games as a coach. Michael Jordan never even entertained coaching because he knew that he did not have the patience to develop players that did not already possess his level of commitment to the craft (Kozlowski, 2020).

No one can question their ability to "do." When it came time to teach others to "do," however, Johnson and Jordan were not up to the task. Their experiences showed that scoring 30 points in an NBA game is easier than teaching someone else to do it. Nevertheless, people find that it is easier to make fun of teaching than to take the time to study the profession and understand that good teachers are good because they possess the brilliance to "do" their area of expertise and get others to do it as well.

In chapter 9, we established that the best teachers function like artists. The difference between, say a painter, and a teacher, is that if a painter creates a beautiful painting, people will know their name. A teacher's works of greatness–the children they influence who do great things in life–do not bear their signature. No one will know of their masterpiece except the teachers and their canvass. Here lies the only reward in teaching: the satisfaction of knowing that you did create a masterpiece. The larger society will never bother to look underneath the frame to see a teacher's signature, but their own work will never forget who is responsible for their creation. The students a teacher reaches will always remember the kindness and time that a good teacher invested in them. Their thanks and gratitude is the only reward for teaching.

As a teacher, their gratitude will never enable you to take the dream vacation you have always wanted. Their thanks will never help you finance the down payment on a modest home. Their love is non-transferable, and you will not be able to exchange it for the luxury car that you have dreamed of owning since you were a kid. You will never be able to barter their appreciation, no matter how much of it you collect, for any good or service. Your reward will likely never come in the form of money, admiration, or even a simple job-well-done pat-on-the-back for all your efforts from your administrative supervisors.

Ultimately, all a teacher will have to show for their hard work is their students' lives, and that, mind you, is no small thing. Perhaps the most memorable day of my career happened when a local organization granted several of my high school students college scholarships. What made the day memorable was that during one of my student's acceptance speech, he mentioned to the audience how much of an impact I had on him as his teacher. Of course, that made me feel great, but the real significance of that day was revealed to me years later when that student told me his backstory. At that event, he was wearing his deceased father's suit that was too big for him, and he had the inside of his shoes lined with plastic shopping bags from Shop-rite to stop water from coming through the holes in the soles of his shoes. That student ultimately graduated from college with a degree in engineering, became a certified math teacher, and then founded a school in Newark, New Jersey. This student's success is the big payday that every teacher dreams of. For a teacher, an Oscar, Pulitzer, or Grammy award could hardly be as valuable as the satisfaction they get from watching one of their students accomplish everything they are capable of despite seemingly impossible odds.

Students are the only thing that makes the whole profession of teaching worthwhile. When a student sincerely tells a teacher that they have had a positive influence on their life, that teacher feels richer than any investment banker could dream. As a teacher, there is no more incredible feeling than to know that you helped someone learn something that they otherwise would never have known and that you helped a person achieve levels of greatness they would never have reached solely on their own. Nothing in the world beats that "teacher-feeling."

It is that teacher-feeling that must sustain teachers when their community denounces the quality of the education their school provides without having done any real research or investigation. This feeling must carry teachers through financial struggles and frustration as they hear people say that teachers are invaluable while resisting even one iota of a tax increase so teachers can have the luxury of both feeding and housing their families. It is this feeling that makes a teacher a real teacher. Nevertheless, they always have to remember that this is all they will ever get. Absolutely no other reward is coming their way for all of their hard work and dedication—nothing.

Great teachers are entirely addicted to this feeling, and that is all they need to keep plugging away even though every logical part of their being tells them to move on to seemingly greener pastures. It helps guide them through times when the path they have chosen seems dark and pointless. Every morning teachers wake up trying to chase that pedagogical high that made them want to become a teacher in the first place, and when they get it, that high reminds them of the hero they are.

Lesson 20: Be Your Own Hero

I end all of my classes the same way, no matter where I am teaching. I think every teacher and parent of Black students must instill this parting advice into their charges' minds: No one is coming to save you. No matter how much you admire Black leaders of the past, none of them will rise from the dead to fix your problems. In the story of Black people's quest for freedom, you are the superhero that saves the day–nobody else is coming to rescue you.

Black students must understand that their access to education gives them obligation, not privilege. Each of them represents millions of Black people

In the story of Black people's quest for freedom, you are the superhero that saves the day–nobody else is coming to rescue you.

across the Diaspora that will never get a chance to have access to the same educational experiences that they have. It is their duty to take the education they obtain and use it to lift someone else. Black students must view their education process as a boot camp that prepares them for the perpetual war to get the world to recognize and accept Black people's humanity.

A crucial component of this fight is Black students understanding that they always have the right to speak their truth as they see it no matter how uncomfortable it makes others feel. I always tell my students that my deepest desire is that they will not try to be loved and admired by present-day American society. If a society inundated with White supremacy, sexism, homophobia, and disdain for the poor loves you, it means you are complicit in the evil that it does. If you are unapologetically standing on the side of justice and freedom, someone, somewhere, is going to despise you. Good. That means that you have said something worth hearing. History does not remember the coward that stood on the sidelines too afraid to get in the game and stand for something. There is no such thing as being neutral in a world in motion. If you watch an elderly person get beaten and robbed, and you do nothing–not even yell for help–you did not stay neutral. You made a conscious decision to help the criminal succeed when you could have easily intervened on the side of justice. Teachers must prepare Black students to show agency and actively shape their society instead of being passively victimized by it.

Given the current state of Black America, there is simply no room for passive spectators. Every Black student need not prepare to be in front of television cameras yelling into a microphone, but every one of them should still have a voice. Teachers and parents have to encourage them to find some corner of the world where their people are hurting and use their knowledge and voice to help because no one is coming to save Black people but themselves.

References

Akbar, N. (1998). Know Thyself. Tallahassee, FL: Mind Productions & Associates.

Akbar, N. (1982). From Miseducation to education. Jersey City, New Jersey: New Mind Productions.

Akbar, N. (1993). Visions for Black men. Nashville, TN: Winston-Derek Publishers.

Americans for the Arts, 2020. Statement On Arts, Jobs, And The Economy. [online] Americans for the Arts. Available at: <https://www.americansforthearts.org/news-room/arts-mobilization-center/statement-on-arts-jobs-and-the-economy> [Accessed 20 September 2020].

Anderson, T. (1992). Introduction to African American studies cultural concepts and theory. Dubuque, Iowa: Kendall/Hunt.

Bekele, S. (2019). *Stop Treating Black Kids Like Criminals - Economic Opportunity Institute.* Economic Opportunity Institute. Retrieved 26 September 2020, from http://www.opportunityinstitute.org/blog/post/stop-treating-black-kids-like-criminals/.

Bidwell, A. (2013). *Lack of Funds Leave School Counselors Struggling to Find BalanceLack of Funds Leave School Counselors Struggling to Find Balance.* U.S. News & World Report. Retrieved 26 September 2020, from https://www.usnews.com/news/articles/2013/09/16/lack-of-funds-leave-school-counselors-struggling-to-find-balance.

Bowman, B., Comer, J., & Johns, D. (2018). Addressing the African American Achievement Gap: Three Leading Educators Issue a Call to Action | NAEYC. Retrieved 22 September 2020, from https://www.naeyc.org/resources/pubs/yc/may2018/achievement-gap

Bryant., H. (2018). The Heritage: Black Athletes, a Divided America, and the Politics of Patriotism. Boston, MA: Beacon Press.

Carmichael, S., & Thelwell, M. (2003). Ready for revolution the life and struggles of Stokely Carmichael (Kwame Ture). New York: Scribner.

Carver-Thomas, D. (2018). *Diversifying the Teaching Profession: How to Recruit and Retain Teachers of Color.* Learningpolicyinstitute.org. Retrieved 4 October 2020, from https://learningpolicyinstitute.org/sites/default/files/product-files/Diversifying_Teaching_Profession_REPORT_0.pdf.

Clarke, J. H. (1995). Who Betrayed the African World Revolution? New York: Third World P.

Chafe, W. H. (2001). Remembering Jim Crow African Americans tell about life in the segregated South. New York: New Press.

Cohen, R. (2014). Monsters: The 1985 Chicago Bears and the Wild Heart of Football. New York: Farrar, Straus and Giroux.

Danzer, G. A. (2002). The Americans. Evanston, IL: McDougal Littell.

Dwyer, K. (2015). *Recalling the day that Magic Johnson decided to destroy Vlade Divac's pager*. Sports.yahoo.com. Retrieved 30 September 2020, from https:// sports.yahoo.com/recalling-the-day-that-magic-johnson-decided-to-destroy-vlade-divac-s-pager-203855976.html? y20=1.

Edsal, L. (2019, August 09). Why Teachers Leave: What the Data Say. Retrieved September 18, 2020, from https:// www.educationevolving.org/blog/2019/02/why-teachers-leave-what-data-say

Epstein, R., Blake, J., & Gonzalez, T. (2019). Girlhood Interrupted: The Erasure of Black Girls' Childhood. Retrieved 12 September 2020, from https:// www.law.georgetown.edu/poverty-inequality-center/wp-content/uploads/sites/14/2017/08/girlhood-interrupted.pdf

Evanzz, K. (1999). The messenger the rise and fall of Elijah Muhammad. New York: Pantheon Books.

Franklin, J. H., & Moss, A. A. (1994). From slavery to freedom a history of African Americans. New York: McGraw-Hill.

Gates, H. L. (1987). The Classic slave narratives. New York: New American Library.

Gilmore, G. E. (1996). Gender and Jim Crow women and the politics of white supremacy in North Carolina, 1896-1920. Chapel Hill: University of North Carolina Press.

Ginzburg, R. (1988). 100 years of lynchings. Baltimore, MD: Black Classic Press.

Guevara, C. (2019). *Drug Detection Dogs in Schools: Are They Worth It? | Drugs in American Society.* Scholarblogs.emory.edu. Retrieved 26 September 2020, from https://scholarblogs.emory.edu/drugsinamericansociety/2019/12/10/drug-detection-dogs-in-schools-are-they-worth-it/.

Henderson, J. (2012). Why Attending Law School Is The Worst Career Decision You'll Ever Make. Retrieved 22 September 2020, from https://www.forbes.com/sites/jmaureenhenderson/2012/06/26/why-attending-law-school-is-the-worst-career-decision-youll-ever-make/#4e36a59044d2

Karenga. (1993). Introduction to Black studies. Los Angeles: University of Sankore Press.

Kerr-Dineen, L. (2016). *Here are your odds of becoming a professional athlete (they're not good).* For The Win. Retrieved 2 October 2020, from https://ftw.usatoday.com/2016/07/here-are-your-odds-of-becoming-a-professional-athlete-theyre-not-good.

Kozlowski, J. (2020). *Michael Jordan's Lack of Patience Kept Him From Ever Becoming a Basketball Coach - Sportscasting | Pure Sports*. Sportscasting | Pure Sports. Retrieved 30 September 2020, from https://www.sportscasting.com/michael-jordans-lack-of-patience-kept-him-from-ever-becoming-a-basketball-coach/.

Kunjufu, J. (1995). Countering the conspiracy to destroy Black boys series. Chicago, Ill: African American Images.

Kunjufu, J. (2002). Black students-Middle class teachers. Chicago, Ill: African American Images.

Ladson-Billings, G. (2006). It's Not the Culture of Poverty, It's the Poverty of Culture: The Problem with Teacher Education. Anthropology and Education Quarterly, 37(2), 104-110.

Lakoff, G. (2014). The ALL NEW Don't Think of an Elephant!: Know Your Values and Frame the Debate (10th ed.). White River Junction, VT: Chelsea Green Publishing.

McDowell, J., 2020. *Rules Without Relationships Lead To Rebellion - Josh.Org*. [online] Josh.org. Available at: <https://www.josh.org/ddl-video/rules-without-relationships-lead-to-rebellion/> [Accessed 19 September 2020].

Moss, J. (2016). *Where Are All the Teachers of Color?*. Harvard Ed. Magazine. Retrieved 4 October 2020, from https://

www.gse.harvard.edu/news/ed/16/05/where-are-all-teachers-color.

National Center for Education Statistics. (2020). The Condition of Education - Preprimary, Elementary, and Secondary Education - Teachers and Staff - Characteristics of Public School Teachers - Indicator May (2020). Retrieved 11 September 2020, from https://nces.ed.gov/programs/coe/indicator_clr.asp

Nilsson, J. (2020). Albert Einstein: "Imagination Is More Important Than Knowledge" | The Saturday Evening Post. Retrieved 21 September 2020, from https://www.saturdayeveningpost.com/2010/03/imagination-important-knowledge/

Oliva, P. F. (2005). Developing the curriculum. New York: Longman.

Oshinsky, D. M. (1996). Worse than slavery Parchman Farm and the ordeal of Jim Crow justice. New York: Free Press.

Packard, J. M. (2002). American nightmare the history of Jim Crow. New York: St. Martin's Press.

Pitre, A., Ray, R., & Pitre, E. (2008). The Struggle for Black History : Foundations for a Critical Black Pedagogy in Education. New York: University P of America, Incorporated.

Rodney, W. (1981). How Europe underdeveloped Africa. Washington, D.C: Howard University Press.

Simpson, C., & Pearlman, A. (2005). Inside the Crips life inside L.A.'s most notorious gang. New York: St. Martin's Press.

Sitrin, C. (2020). *Proposed cuts to New Jersey school-based mental health services 'unconscionable,' educators say.* Politico PRO. Retrieved 26 September 2020, from https://www.politico.com/states/new-jersey/story/2020/09/01/proposed-cuts-to-school-based-mental-health-services-unconscionable-educators-say-1314114.

Spencer, M. B., Noll, E., Stoltzfus, J., & Harpalani, V. (2001). Identity and School Adjustment: Revisiting the "Acting White" Assumption. EDUCATIONAL PSYCHOLOGIST, 36(1), 21-30.

Stampp, K. M. (1956). The peculiar institution. New York: Knopf.

Stewart, J. C. (1996). 1001 things everyone should know about African-American history. New York: Doubleday.

Stumacher, A. (2020). *Opinion | The Man Behind the Metal Detector.* Nytimes.com. Retrieved 26 September 2020, from https://www.nytimes.com/2017/04/29/opinion/sunday/the-man-behind-the-metal-detector.html.

Tobin, S. (Director). (2005, January 03). Money Makeovers [Television series episode]. In The Dr. Phil Show. Los Angeles, California: CBS.

Walker, C. E. (1992). "When I Can Read My Title Clear": Literacy, Slavery, and Religion in the Antebellum South. The Journal of American History, 79, 262-264.

Williamson, J. (1986). A rage for order Black/White relations in the American South since emancipation. New York: Oxford University Press.

Wilson, A. N. (1993). The falsification of Afrikan consciousness Eurocentric history, psychiatry, and the politics of white supremacy. New York: Afrikan World InfoSystems.

WNYC News. (2016). Kids in Prison: Getting Tried as An Adult Depends on Skin Color | WNYC | New York Public Radio, Podcasts, Live Streaming Radio, News. Retrieved 12 September 2020, from https://www.wnyc.org/story/black-kids-more-likely-be-tried-adults-cant-be-explained/

Woodson, C. G. (1933). The mis-education of the Negro. Washington, D.C.: The Associated publishers, inc."

Young, Y. (2020). Teachers' implicit bias against black students starts in preschool, study finds. Retrieved 11 September 2020, from https://www.theguardian.com/world/2016/oct/04/black-students-teachers-implicit-racial-bias-preschool-study

ABOUT THE AUTHOR

Joel I. Plummer earned a B.A. in African and African American Studies, an M.A. in history, and was inducted into Phi Beta Kappa at Rutgers University-Newark. He earned a Supervisor of Instruction Certificate through the Rutgers University Graduate School of Education. He has taught African American and U.S. history for more than two decades at the secondary level and currently teaches in the Africana Studies department at Rutgers University in New Brunswick, New Jersey.

In addition to teaching, Joel I. Plummer has worked as a photojournalist for more than a decade. The Los Angeles Times, The Wall Street Journal, The Daily Beast, Newsweek, NBC, CBS, Sports Illustrated, ESPN, and numerous international media outlets have published his work. He is a product of the Plainfield Public School District in New Jersey, is a member of Iota Phi Theta Fraternity, Inc., and still lives in Plainfield with his wife, Danielle, and their children, Alexis, Morgan, and Mason.